BEDFORD COLLEGE EDITIONS

Herman Melville

Benito Cereno

Edited by Wyn Kelley
Massachusetts Institute of Technology

Bedford/St. Martin's
BOSTON • NEW YORK

For Bedford/St. Martin's

EXECUTIVE EDITOR: Stephen A. Scipione
ASSOCIATE EDITOR: Amy Hurd Gershman
SENIOR PRODUCTION SUPERVISOR: Joe Ford
PRODUCTION ASSOCIATE: Maureen O'Neill
PROJECT MANAGEMENT: Books By Design, Inc.
TEXT DESIGN: Judith Arisman/Arisman Design Studio
COVER DESIGN: Donna L. Dennison
COVER ART: E. A. Renard, *Rébellion d'un esclave sur un navrire
negrier*. 1833. Museé du Nouveau Monde.
COMPOSITION: Macmillan India, Ltd.
PRINTING AND BINDING: RR Donnelley & Sons Company

PRESIDENT: Joan E. Feinberg
EDITORIAL DIRECTOR: Denise B. Wydra
EDITOR IN CHIEF: Karen S. Henry
DIRECTOR OF MARKETING: Karen Melton Soeltz
DIRECTOR OF EDITING, DESIGN, AND PRODUCTION: Marcia Cohen
MANAGER, PUBLISHING SERVICES: Emily Berleth

Library of Congress Control Number: 2005936611

For information, write: Bedford/St. Martin's, 75 Arlington Street,
Boston, MA 02116   (617-399-4000)

ISBN-10: 0-312-45242-X
ISBN-13: 978-0-312-45242-1

Acknowledgments
Photograph of Herman Melville, 1860, on page 1. Courtesy Berkshire Athenaeum,
Pittsfield, Massachusetts.

Preface

ABOUT THE SERIES

THE BEDFORD COLLEGE EDITIONS reprint enduring literary works in a handsome, readable, and affordable format. The text of each work is lightly but helpfully annotated. Prepared by eminent scholars and teachers, the editorial matter in each volume includes a chronology of the life of the author; an illustrated introduction to the contexts and major issues of the text in its time and ours; an annotated bibliography for further reading (contexts, criticism, and Internet resources); and a concise glossary of literary terms. The text of the work is also accessible online at an accompanying Web site (visit *bedfordstmartins.com/americanlit*), where it can be searched electronically.

ABOUT THIS VOLUME

Using the Northwestern-Newberry text, which collates the 1855 and 1856 publications of *The Piazza Tales* as its source, this edition of *Benito Cereno* includes a survey of Herman Melville's life and writing and contextualizes the story in terms of literary genres and influences, historical and political events, and issues of audience and performance that have arisen in strenuous critical debate over Melville's work since the mid-twentieth century. An introduction lays out the history of the text and its reception and shows how fully Melville responded to a culture in turmoil over the Compromise of 1850, New World colonialism, and the expansion of slavery into new territories. Addressing themes made popular by Nathaniel Hawthorne, Frederick Douglass, and Harriet Beecher Stowe, Melville produced a story that continues to raise questions about issues at the heart of American culture. The introduction also shows how *Benito Cereno* came to be considered one of the most subtle and intriguing of Melville's short stories: a true masterwork.

As subtle and intriguing as Melville's story is, it is also a rewriting of an earlier text, Amasa Delano's *A Narrative of Voyages and Travels in the Northern and Southern Hemispheres* (1817). Melville characteristically reworked travel narratives and histories, and we lose an important dimension of his aesthetic practice when we read them out of their literary context. This edition includes the chapter in Delano's narrative that formed the basis of Melville's plot and characters and provided the legal documents that Melville appended, with little revision, to the end of his story. A close study of Delano's chapter reveals how imaginatively Melville worked with his sources.

NOTE ON THE TEXT

Benito Cereno originally appeared in *Putnam's Monthly Magazine* (October 1855, 353–67; November 1855, 459–74; December 1855, 633–44). It was later published as part of a collection, *The Piazza Tales* (New York: Dix & Edwards, 1856). The authoritative edition at present is *The Piazza Tales and Other Prose Pieces, 1839–1860*, edited by Harrison Hayford, Alma A. McDougall, and G. Thomas Tanselle, in *The Writings of Herman Melville*, Vol. 9, edited by Harrison Hayford, Hershel Parker, and G. Thomas Tanselle (Evanston and Chicago: Northwestern UP and the Newberry Library, 1987). Each Northwestern-Newberry edition of Melville's texts includes a lengthy Historical Note and a complete list of variants. This is especially important for *Benito Cereno*, which appeared in two different versions during Melville's life. *Benito Cereno* also exists as a theatrical adaptation in Joyce Sparer Adler's *Dramatization of Three Melville Novels* (New York: Mellen, 1992).

Spellings throughout reflect nineteenth-century practices and may be inconsistent.

ACKNOWLEDGMENTS

I am immensely grateful to Susan Belasco and Linck Johnson, editors of *The Bedford Anthology of American Literature*, for inviting me to edit this volume, and to Steve Scipione for his subtle and acute editing of the manuscript. The staff at Bedford/St. Martin's has been uncommonly helpful, especially Emily Berleth and Amy Hurd Gershman, and Alison Fields of Books By Design. I would like to thank Jay Fliegelman for his superb reading of the manuscript and his advice and encouragement. I have also benefited enormously from fellow scholars and friends whose work has opened my eyes: Charlene Avallone, Dennis Berthold, Hester Blum, John Bryant, Wai Chee Dimock, Mahni Ghorashi, Henry Hughes, Carolyn Karcher, Robert S. Levine, Timothy Marr, Samuel Otter, Laurie Robertson-Lorant, John Stauffer, and Ellen Weinauer. My colleagues in the Melville Society Cultural Project—Jill Barnum, Mary K. Bercaw Edwards, Elizabeth Schultz, Christopher Sten, and Robert K. Wallace—directly inspired my thinking, and I thank Robert K. Wallace for his close reading of the manuscript as well. Britt Peterson advised me on a significant point. I can never adequately acknowledge the love and support of Dale, Britt, and Bayne Peterson.

Wyn Kelley

Contents

Chronology:
The Life of Herman Melville

1791-1804 Haitian revolution. Toussaint L'Ouverture (ca. 1743-1803) leads the revolt and eventually becomes a general and governor of Haiti.

1805 Amasa Delano, captain of the *Perseverance*, encounters Benito Cereno, captain of the *Tryal*, near the island of Santa María off Chile.

1817 Publication of Amasa Delano's *A Narrative of Voyages and Travels, in the Northern and Southern Hemispheres*.

1819 Birth of Herman Melville (Figure 1) on August 1 in New York City, third child of Allan Melvill and Maria Gansevoort Melvill.

1830 Family moves to Albany when Allan's business debts mount. Allan's friend Lemuel Shaw becomes chief justice of the Massachusetts Supreme Court.

1831 Nat Turner's slave revolt put down in Virginia.

1832	Allan Melvill, in desperate financial straits, dies of fever. Herman becomes a bank clerk. Maria Melvill adds an "e" to the family name.
1837	After working in his brother Gansevoort's store, Herman takes a teaching job close to Pittsfield, Massachusetts, where an uncle lives. Nathaniel Hawthorne (1804-1864) publishes *Twice-Told Tales.*
1838	Melville family moves to Lansingburgh, New York.
1839	Melville publishes two magazine sketches. Works on a merchant ship, the *St. Lawrence*, sailing to Liverpool and back. *Amistad* revolt, led by Joseph Cinque, or Sengbe Pieh.
1840	After brief teaching jobs, Melville seeks work in Illinois with his friend Eli James Murdock Fly. After unsuccessful attempts at finding employment, travels to New Bedford, Massachusetts, where Frederick Douglass (1818?-1895) is working on the wharves and active in local churches and abolitionist groups. Melville signs on the *Acushnet*, a whaling ship.
1841	*Creole* revolt, led by Madison Washington.
1841-1844	Melville sails from Fairhaven, Massachusetts, January 3, 1841. In 1842, in Nuku Hiva (Marquesas Islands), jumps ship and travels with a friend, Richard Tobias Greene, into the interior, where he supposedly* spends four weeks living as a captive among the Taipi. Escapes to the bay and joins the crew of another whaling ship, the *Lucy Ann*. The crew mutinies in Tahiti, where Melville goes ashore and is briefly confined. Serves on the *Charles and Henry*, another whaling ship, until discharged in the Sandwich Islands (Hawai'i) in 1843. Works at odd jobs before signing on a naval vessel, the *United States*, and sailing home. Arrives in Boston in October 1844.
1845	Douglass publishes his *Narrative of the Life of Frederick Douglass, an American Slave.*
1846	Melville publishes *Typee*, an account of his sojourn among the Marquesans. Hawthorne publishes a collection of tales, *Mosses from an Old Manse.*
1847	Melville publishes *Omoo*, a sequel to *Typee*, based on his visit to Tahiti. In August, marries Elizabeth Shaw, daughter of Lemuel Shaw. Lives in New York City and participates in the Young America literary movement, a group of writers and editors committed to establishing an American literary culture independent of European models.
1848	Douglass publishes an excerpt from *Typee* in his journal, *North Star.*

* New research indicates we don't know this for sure.

1849   Melville publishes *Mardi,* a philosophical and political romance set in an imaginary Pacific archipelago. Poor reviews and the birth of a son, Malcolm, drive him to attempt more saleable books. Publishes *Redburn,* an account of a young man's trip to Liverpool, based on his 1839 voyage. Travels to London and Europe to market the book to publishers abroad. Douglass gives an oration, "Slavery, the Slumbering Volcano," in New York City.

1850   Compromise of 1850 includes the Fugitive Slave Act, which guarantees that slaves escaping to free states may be returned to their masters. Melville publishes *White-Jacket,* based on his naval service. Hawthorne publishes *The Scarlet Letter.* On a visit to the Berkshires in Massachusetts, Melville writes an enthusiastic review, "Hawthorne and His Mosses," meets Hawthorne, and establishes a close friendship. Moves his family to a farm, Arrowhead, just outside Lenox, Massachusetts. Begins rewriting *Moby-Dick* under the influence of what he calls in his dedication Hawthorne's "genius."

1851   Publication of *Moby-Dick* to a disappointing reception. Birth of second child, Stanwix. Douglass publishes "The Heroic Slave," based on the *Creole* revolt. Lemuel Shaw rules in the case of Thomas Sims, escaped slave, and orders him returned to his master. Hawthorne moves his family from the Berkshires to West Newton, Massachusetts, and later, in 1852, to Concord, Massachusetts.

1852   Publication of a domestic romance, *Pierre, or The Ambiguities,* to disastrous reviews. Harriet Beecher Stowe (1811-1896) publishes *Uncle Tom's Cabin* to enormous acclaim. Hawthorne publishes *The Blithedale Romance* and a campaign biography of Franklin Pierce, which results in his receiving a political appointment to the consulate of Liverpool. Melville proposes to Hawthorne that he write the story of Agatha Hatch, a wronged wife, based on notes Melville made after a visit to Nantucket with Lemuel Shaw. Hawthorne returns the materials to Melville, who writes *Isle of the Cross* (now lost); submits it to *Harper's* in 1853 and is rejected. Belatedly applies for a consulship but is unsuccessful.

1853   Hawthorne departs for Liverpool. Birth of Melville's third child, Elizabeth. Melville accepts invitations from *Putnam's Monthly Magazine* and *Harper's New Monthly Magazine,* writing sixteen stories over three years and having most of them published.

1854   *Frederick Douglass' Paper* prints an excerpt from *Moby-Dick* and an enthusiastic notice of a serial installment of Melville's *Israel Potter,* a historical novel about a Revolutionary War soldier.

1855	Publication of *Benito Cereno* in *Putnam's*. Birth of fourth child, Frances. Publication of *Israel Potter*. Douglass publishes his second autobiography, *My Bondage and My Freedom*.
1856	Melville collects five of his magazine stories, including *Benito Cereno*; writes a prefatory sketch, "The Piazza"; and publishes the collection as *The Piazza Tales*. Completes the manuscript of *The Confidence-Man* and travels to Europe in October on an extended trip to recover his failing health. Visits Hawthorne in Liverpool.
1857	Continues his travels to the Mediterranean, Egypt, Greece, and the Holy Land. *The Confidence-Man* is published in April.
1857–1860	Writes poetry, some of it based on his travels. Makes three lecture tours, on the topics of "Statues in Rome," "The South Seas," and "Traveling." Tries unsuccessfully to publish a book of poems. Travels in 1860 to San Francisco with his brother Thomas, a ship captain, but returns to New York alone after a difficult voyage.
1861	The Civil War begins. Melville tries to obtain another consulship but fails. Lemuel Shaw dies.
1862	A fall from his wagon causes severe injury and drives him and his family to consider moving back to New York City.
1863	Returns to New York and lives at 104 East Twenty-sixth Street.
1864	Travels to Civil War battlefields and takes part in a raid that becomes the source of a poem, "The Scout toward Aldie." Hawthorne dies.
1866	Publication of *Battle-Pieces and Aspects of the War*, a collection of commemorative poems on the Civil War. Wins a political appointment as district inspector in the Customs Service in New York. Continues actively writing poems.
1867	Son Malcolm commits suicide.
1876	Publication of a verse epic, *Clarel*, a story of a young theological student's journey to Jerusalem and its environs.
1885	Resigns from the Customs Service after nineteen years of service.
1886	Stanwix dies in San Francisco.
1888	Publication of *John Marr and Other Sailors*, a collection of verse reminiscences of the sea. Begins manuscript of *Billy Budd*, which starts as a verse narrative like others in *John Marr* but develops into a novella.
1891	Compiles a manuscript of poems, "Weeds and Wildings," and privately publishes *Timoleon*, including a number of poems related to his European travels. Continues revising *Billy Budd* but does not finish. Dies September 28.

An Introduction to *Benito Cereno*

Benito Cereno is one of the most powerful and mysterious stories of nineteenth-century American literature. But when Herman Melville (1819-1891) published it in three installments of *Putnam's Monthly Magazine* (October, November, and December 1855), he could hardly have anticipated that a century and a half later, it would rival his masterpiece *Moby-Dick* (1851), notable stories such as "Bartleby, the Scrivener" (1853) and *Billy Budd* (1891), and his many lesser-known novels, stories, and poems as a work appreciated by readers all over the world. Although it received only modest attention when it appeared and was read well into the twentieth century as a minor work attesting to Melville's concerns with moral absolutes of good and evil, it is now considered one of his finest stories, a pinnacle of his literary treatments of the sea and maritime history, and one of the nineteenth century's most subtle probings of European colonialism and American slavery.

The Melville who wrote *Benito Cereno* was a very different author from the Melville familiar to us from *Moby-Dick*, even though the story appeared only four years after his celebrated novel. At the time he finished his great whaling adventure in 1851, he described his early life in a letter to Nathaniel Hawthorne as one steady "unfolding." His authorial career to date had been brief – only five years – and, with six novels in that short time, unutterably intense. He seemed, as he told Hawthorne, "like one of those seeds taken out of the Egyptian Pyramids, which after being three thousand years a seed and nothing but a seed, being planted in English soil, it developed itself, grew to greenness, and then fell to mould." At thirty-two and seemingly at the height of his powers, Melville thought he had "come to the inmost leaf of the bulb, and that shortly the flower must fall" (June 1?, 1851; NN *Corr* 193).

Melville may have felt that he had reached his limits as a writer because he was running out of the firsthand maritime experiences that had up until then provided material for all his novels. Melville was born into a well-placed middle-class family in New York City. His father, Allan Melvill, was an importer of European textiles and fancy dress goods and the son of a Revolutionary War major, Thomas Melvill, who had participated in the Boston Tea Party. His mother, Maria Gansevoort Melvill (she added an "e" to the name in 1832), was descended from Dutch Albany patricians who had owned slaves. When his father's business failed and he died in 1832, Melville, the third of eight children and the second son, had to end his education and go to work as a bank clerk. In 1839, at the age of nineteen, he shipped out on a merchant vessel bound for Liverpool, getting his first taste of the sea – and the basis for his 1849 novel *Redburn.* After various unsuccessful attempts at schoolteaching, farming, and looking for work on the Erie Canal, he followed in the footsteps of his nautical cousins, several of whom had served in the navy, and went to sea as a whaler – perhaps the most bloody, exhausting, poorly paid work in America's shipping trades. His ship, the *Acushnet*, departed from Fairhaven, Massachusetts, on January 3, 1841. Melville would not return until 1844, by which time he had accumulated an abundant stock of nautical yarns.

In the most sensational of these tales, Melville and a friend, Richard Tobias Greene, jumped ship at Nuku Hiva in the Marquesas Islands, fled into an interior valley, and stumbled upon the villages of the Taipi, where they apparently stayed for several weeks as captives. After escaping, Melville signed on with another whaling ship, the *Lucy Ann*, which was so badly managed that he mutinied with most of the crew and was put ashore in Tahiti to languish in a makeshift barracks. Escaping this confinement too, he enjoyed a few weeks of beachcombing before signing on with a Nantucket whaler, the *Charles and Henry*, which took him to the Sandwich Islands (Hawai'i). Discharged from his ship and taking odd jobs onshore, Melville passed three months before enlisting in the U.S. Navy and sailing home on the *United States*.

That was the point from which, Melville told Hawthorne, "I date my life." He initiated his writing with *Typee* (1846), an account of his sojourn among the Marquesans. His portrayal of tattooed islanders, alluring maidens, cannibalism, and taboo rituals titillated readers eager for sensational travel accounts and made him an overnight success. He followed it quickly with a sequel, *Omoo* (1847), based on his rovings in Tahiti. Shortly thereafter, he married Elizabeth Shaw, daughter of Lemuel Shaw, the chief justice of the Massachusetts Supreme Court. The young couple moved to New York City, where Melville became active in the Young America movement, which aimed to establish a new American literature to compete with the literary dominance of Europe. Melville's raised ambitions appear in his next book, *Mardi* (1849). Beginning on a whaling ship, the story takes its protagonist, Taji, on an extended tour through an imaginary Pacific archipelago, where each island, like the legendary domains of Jonathan Swift's *Gulliver's Travels*, represents a version of European or American civilization. Like his other two novels, *Mardi* satirizes Western culture while idealizing the Pacific idyll and Melville's own philosophical and lyrical flights of fancy.

With the birth of a son in 1849, and with *Mardi* only moderately successful, Melville turned to more realistic and saleable narratives, quickly producing *Redburn* (1849), based on the Liverpool voyage, and *White-Jacket* (1850), founded on his service in the navy. He then started a story about whaling, the one subject he had not previously explored in depth. He might have produced a nautical adventure like his earlier works had he not met Nathaniel Hawthorne in the summer of 1850. This meeting and the men's subsequent friendship galvanized Melville. He moved his family to the Berkshires to be closer to Hawthorne and the community of writers and artists who flourished in the vicinity of Lenox and Pittsfield, Massachusetts. There he recommenced *Moby-Dick*, feeling for the first time the freedom to write of the metaphysical ideas and symbols that he identified in Hawthorne as a "power of blackness": the commitment, as he put it in *Moby-Dick*, to "preach the Truth to the face of Falsehood!" (*MD* 48). Melville's letters to Hawthorne reveal that the experience of writing *Moby-Dick* unleashed in him a fury of words and ideas, expanding his literary reach to radically new horizons.

Within just four years, the picture of Melville's career had dramati-
cally changed. Hawthorne left the Berkshires in 1851, and the reviews of
Moby-Dick were deeply disappointing. With a second son born in 1851 and
two daughters following in 1853 and 1855, and with payments due on loans
he had taken out for his farm, Arrowhead, Melville needed to recapture his
early success. Hoping to appeal to the thriving market in sentimental
romance, Melville turned for his next novel to a story of love and marriage:
Pierre, or the Ambiguities (1852). Unfortunately, the beautiful, romantic couple he portrayed were also brother and sister. Incest was hardly an accept-
able subject for mid-nineteenth-century readers, and the novel received
disastrous reviews. It appeared that Melville's career as a novelist had run
its course.

Melville faced this discouraging news during a particularly tense political season that culminated in the election of President Franklin Pierce, a college friend of Hawthorne's. Pierce won on a platform upholding the
Compromise of 1850, which extended slavery into territories gained by the
Mexican War and strengthened the existing Fugitive Slave Law to empower
southern slaveholders to recapture escaped slaves, even if they fled to free
states. Chief Justice Shaw, Melville's father-in-law, judged the case of Thomas
Sims (1851) under the new law and returned him to his master. Having
endured captivity himself in different forms as a sailor and whaleman, and
also having worked alongside seamen of many races and nations, Melville
had satirized American slave owners in his earlier works. The year 1852 must
have seemed a calamity to him, not only in terms of his personal career but
also in the political landscape of compromise over slavery.

Hawthorne shared many of Melville's doubts about the political climate
in 1852, but, building on his connection with Pierce, he wrote a successful
campaign biography of the candidate and won a political appointment, the
consulship of Liverpool, after Pierce's election. Melville had thoughts of
applying for such an appointment too, but they came to nothing. In the
meantime, he had been solicited by two new journals in New York – *Putnam's
Monthly Magazine* and *Harper's New Monthly Magazine* – to write articles
and stories. In 1853, he began publishing the first of eventually sixteen
stories, as well as a serialized historical narrative, *Israel Potter*, published
as a novel in 1855. In these works, his subject was less the sea and sailors
than the working men and women he encountered in New York and the
Berkshires: the copyist Bartleby, the factory women of "The Paradise of
Bachelors and the Tartarus of Maids," and the rural laborer Merrymusk of
"Cock-A-Doodle-Doo!" "The Encantadas" is a series of sketches about the
Galápagos Islands and the pirates and castaways who occasionally touched

their shores. "The Bell-Tower" and *Israel Potter* signal his interest in historical subjects. *Benito Cereno* appeared in *Putnam's* in installments in 1855. It is hard to generalize about such a wide-ranging collection of fiction, but in a broad sense, the author of *Benito Cereno* was a more controlled writer than the author of *Moby-Dick*. In place of the exuberant storyteller who grabs the reader's attention – "Call me Ishmael" – and subjects him or her to rhapsodies of language and philosophy, *Benito Cereno* offers a noticeably masked narrator. Melville's short stories, working within their compressed spaces, produced some of his most intricately designed, subtly allusive, and often puzzling fiction. One can see the effects of this development in his last novel, *The Confidence-Man* (1857), published shortly after his collection of magazine fiction, *The Piazza Tales* (1856). In this novel, the confidence-man, a shape-shifting figure, makes his way through the shady world aboard a Mississippi River steamboat. Here and elsewhere in Melville's later fiction, nothing is quite as it seems.

It was a twentieth-century commonplace to think of Melville's short works and *The Confidence-Man* as the last gasps of an exhausted author. Although they earned him a competent living, he never regained his early reputation, and his later turn to lyceum lectures (1857-1860) and especially to writing poems for the next thirty years was seen as a falling off from his novels. In spite of his having published a substantial collection of Civil War verse, *Battle-Pieces and Aspects of the War* (1866); a massive verse narrative, *Clarel* (1876), based on his travels in the Mediterranean and Holy Land; and two late collections of poems, Melville was until recently seen as a failed novelist more than an innovative, challenging, and successful poet. His late manuscript, the novella *Billy Budd*, left unfinished at his death and first published in 1924, has been viewed as the final legacy of a most unusual career.

Because of its concern with slavery, *Benito Cereno* has recently achieved a more prominent place in that career, as readers have become more interested in treatments of race in American literature. It is important to remember, though, that to Melville's first readers, *Benito Cereno* – with its nautical setting, rich verbal texture, and pastiche of fiction and documents, fable and reality – might have appeared to be in line with his earlier accounts combining travel, history, philosophy, fact, and fantasy in the sort of narrative stew that captivated mid-nineteenth-century urbanites. In the tale of a well-meaning American captain, Amasa Delano (Figure 1), who rescues a Spanish ship with a cargo of African slaves off the coast of Chile and succors its captain, Benito Cereno, nineteenth-century American magazine readers would have recognized subjects and themes that received considerable attention in such popular journals as *Putnam's*.

Figure 1. Frontispiece from Amasa Delano, *A Narrative of Voyages and Travels, in the Northern and Southern Hemispheres* (Boston: E. G. House, 1817). *Courtesy of the New Bedford Whaling Museum.*

Some of Melville's readers also might have understood that he was working within a habitual mode – namely, using existing historical sources, in this case a chapter from Amasa Delano's *A Narrative of Voyages and Travels, in the Northern and Southern Hemispheres* (1817) (Figure 2). Melville announces his debt to history not only in his references to dates and names in the early paragraphs but also by including legal documents at the end of the narrative that give the "inside" story of Benito Cereno's baffling behavior on board his mysterious ship, the *San Dominick*. In a magazine that included lengthy historical and geographical articles; extended profiles of significant authors, heroes, and statesmen; and substantial travel essays, stories, poems, reviews, and sketches, a reader would customarily experience a mélange of genres and styles. Melville achieves a similar effect in his multigeneric narrative.

Melville's first readers might have expected little more than an entertaining tale of an accidental encounter with a perplexing ship on the high seas and would have surrendered with pleasure to its mysteries. For the

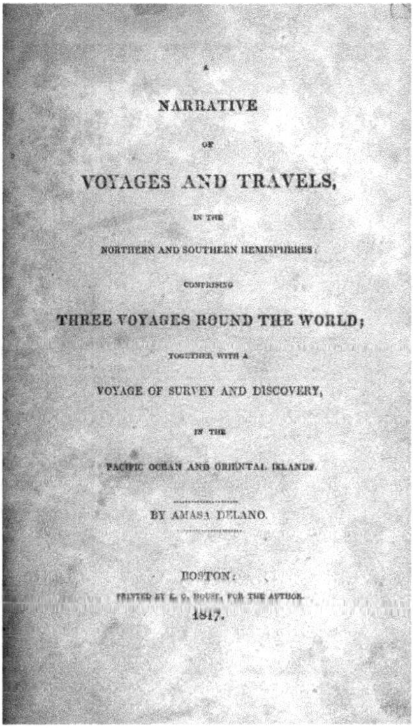
A

NARRATIVE

OF

VOYAGES AND TRAVELS,

IN THE

NORTHERN AND SOUTHERN HEMISPHERES:

COMPRISING

THREE VOYAGES ROUND THE WORLD;

TOGETHER WITH A

VOYAGE OF SURVEY AND DISCOVERY,

IN THE

PACIFIC OCEAN AND ORIENTAL ISLANDS.

BY AMASA DELANO.

BOSTON:

PRINTED BY E. G. HOUSE, FOR THE AUTHOR.

1817.

Figure 2. Facsimile of title page of Amasa Delano, *A Narrative of Voyages and Travels, in the Northern and Southern Hemispheres*. *Courtesy of the New Bedford Whaling Museum.*

twenty-first-century reader, however, some further understanding of Melville's literary context enriches the story considerably. What kind of story is *Benito Cereno*? How is it like or different from other stories of the period? The following sections look at *Benito Cereno* as a historical tale, a slave narrative, and a form of popular theater – the literary forms to which Melville responded most powerfully and drew on most innovatively.

HAWTHORNE, HISTORY, AND THE PIAZZA TALE

After *Benito Cereno* appeared in *Putnam's Monthly Magazine* in 1855, Melville planned a book of his collected stories, but he changed his mind several times about what form it would take. At first he considered a volume titled "Benito Cereno & Other Sketches"; then he proposed a new book called *The Piazza Tales*, in which *Benito Cereno* appeared near the middle.

When Melville moved *Benito Cereno* from its leading position in "Benito Cereno & Other Sketches" to third place in *The Piazza Tales*, he also made an important generic shift. As a sketch, *Benito Cereno* would have fit into the tradition of occasional, reflective, or satirical pieces such as those written by Washington Irving (*The Sketch-Book of Geoffrey Crayon* [1819-1820]), Lydia Maria Child (*Letters from New York* [1843, 1845]), Nathaniel Hawthorne ("The Custom-House" [1850]), or Fanny Fern (*Fern Leaves from Fanny's Port-folio* [1853]). Like these works, it would have been read as an ephemeral piece: probably nonfiction; often dressed with the author's fancy, humor, or stylistic elaboration; and serving to amuse, divert, or instruct. Melville makes it clear that he recognized the generic expectations of the sketch. The ten sketches in one of his stories, "The Encantadas," include a piquant blend of observations, natural history, maritime history, literary allusion, and character studies. Knowing that *Benito Cereno* might be read as a historical sketch, like some of the material in "The Encantadas," he wrote his editors a note explaining its relationship to its source, Amasa Delano's *Narrative*, thus establishing his story's factual basis and presenting it as informative nonfiction (*PT* 581).

Between January 19, 1856, however, when Melville proposed the title and table of contents for "Benito Cereno & Other Sketches," and February 16, when he announced a new title (*The Piazza Tales*), a new "accompanying piece" ("The Piazza"), and a new order, placing *Benito Cereno* after "The Piazza" and "Bartleby," "Benito Cereno" the sketch became *Benito Cereno* the tale. With this move, Melville may have in one sense diminished *Benito Cereno*'s impact on the collection. "The Piazza," with its dreamy evocation of Melville's home in the Berkshires and of the narrator's encounter with a lonely farm girl, Marianna, who sits sewing in a remote cottage, frames *The Piazza Tales* as a compilation of occasional pieces, seemingly removed from the political and social turmoil of mid-nineteenth-century America. By placing *Benito Cereno* after "The Piazza" and "Bartleby," Melville signals that his Spanish captain is simply another odd specimen of humanity, like the lonely sewing girl or forlorn scrivener, a piece of human jetsam picked up on the narrator's travels. Indeed, the mood of dreamy allure that suffuses much of *Benito Cereno* up to the climax seems consistent with the volume's appearance of being a pleasant book to while away an idle afternoon. Reviews of *The Piazza Tales* called it "a delightful companion for an afternoon lounge" and stressed its "taking variety of style," "its art of conveying deep expression by simple touches," and "that peculiar richness of language, descriptive vitality, and splendidly somber imagination which are the author's characteristics" (*PT* 504, 502).

It was in just such terms, however, that Hawthorne's and Irving's tales were typically described, and it seems likely that Melville modeled his style on their work, especially Hawthorne's *Twice-Told Tales* (1837, 1851) and *Mosses from an Old Manse* (1846, 1854). Melville wrote an enthusiastic review, "Hawthorne and His Mosses," near the time of meeting the author in 1850. He read *Twice-Told Tales* with great pleasure in February 1851, telling his friend Evert Duyckinck, "I think they far exceed the 'Mosses' – they are, I fancy, an earlier vintage from his vine. Some of those sketches are wonderfully subtle. Their deeper meanings are worthy of a Brahmin." Although Melville expressed some reservations about Hawthorne, he maintained the utmost admiration for him: "Nevertheless, for one, I regard Hawthorne (in his books) as evincing a quality of genius, immensely loftier, & more profound, too, than any other American has shown hitherto in the printed form. Irving is a grasshopper to him" (*Corr* 181).

Hawthorne wrote many different kinds of tales, but the ones Melville especially admired in "Hawthorne and His Mosses" suggest what he had in mind for *The Piazza Tales*. Of the two he chose for particular praise – "A Select Party" and "Young Goodman Brown" – the first is an example of the sort of fanciful sketch that Hawthorne perfected. "A Select Party" describes a gathering of notables at a castle in the sky created for the occasion by the Man of Fancy, who entertains visitors like the Oldest Inhabitant, Monsieur On-Dit ("They-Say"), and the Clerk of the Weather. His most cherished guest, the Master Genius, looks quite a bit like Hawthorne and resembles the type of new American author that Melville championed in "Mosses" and that the Young America movement prized. "Young Goodman Brown" receives even deeper praise, representing as it does the "power of blackness" (*PT* 243) that Melville found so bewitching in Hawthorne. In spite of the misleadingly simple title, "Young Goodman Brown" appeared to Melville as "deep as Dante" (*PT* 251), an example of the "flashings-forth of the intuitive Truth" (*PT* 244) that marked Shakespeare, and now this great American author, as a genius.

On the basis of "Young Goodman Brown" and his many other narratives of colonial American history, including his acknowledged masterpiece *The Scarlet Letter* (1850), Hawthorne was celebrated among his contemporaries as the premier interpreter of America's legendary past. His historical fiction probed the "darkness" of that past, especially the burden of patriarchal authority that Puritan and colonial fathers pressed upon young men and women in a post-Revolutionary era. Although Hawthorne makes few or only oblique references to slavery in his work, his fixation on national sin probably encouraged Melville's exploration of the dark side of American democracy, progress, and freedom in *Benito Cereno*. Melville's historical fiction, *Israel Potter*, based on the life of a Revolutionary War soldier who becomes a casualty of American democracy, shares with Hawthorne's work, especially "My Kinsman, Major Molineux," an ironic view of the country's promises of freedom and opportunity for ordinary Americans.

As if to contain the rebellious energies of his politically subversive wit, Hawthorne packaged his stories in eminently marketable volumes that proclaimed his domestic concerns and sentimental leanings. His preface to *The Scarlet Letter* gives a prime example of concerted political satire – on the Whigs who removed him from the Custom-House in Salem – couched in dreamy musings on romance, moonlight, the Actual, and the Imaginary. The two stories Melville selected from *Mosses* display Hawthorne's bipolar literary tendencies handily. Melville's choice, then, to lodge the explosive and threatening *Benito Cereno* at the heart of a charming book called *The Piazza Tales* seems to reflect what he learned from Hawthorne. Referring to a piazza, or porch, built on the north side of Arrowhead, Melville's title gestures toward Hawthorne's tales written from *his* house, the Old Manse in Concord.

Melville's prefatory sketch, "The Piazza," is brief and appears to be autobiographical, based on Melville's efforts at home improvement. Around that fact, Melville's narrator weaves a fanciful narrative of traveling to see what he imagines, from his piazza view, to be a fairy cottage, not too different from Hawthorne's cloud castle in "A Select Party." When he arrives, he finds the lonely sewing girl, Marianna, instead. Though poor and neglected, she draws comfort from looking down from her mountaintop upon a dwelling that she imagines as King Charming's palace, but which the narrator is startled to see is his own farmhouse. Not disabusing her of her romantic dream, and not offering to relieve her poverty either, he withdraws to his piazza and anticipates watching the opera of nature from his "box-royal," his privileged seat of leisure.

The narrator ends the story with a sober reflection on his experience: "But, every night, when the curtain falls, truth comes in with darkness. No light shows from the mountain. To and fro, I walk the piazza deck, haunted by Marianna's face, and many as real a story" (*PT* 12). With this conclusion, Melville introduces his collection of "real" stories and suggests that what follows may resemble Hawthorne's tales in offering a feast of various literary dishes seasoned with social criticism and irony and garnished with romantic flourishes. But what does Melville really mean by a piazza tale? It depends on how you define *piazza*. In the story and in actuality at Arrowhead, it is a porch, a word derived from the Latin *porticus* and denoting a covered outside structure attached to a house. For most of the story, the narrator's piazza is a place "somehow combining the coziness of in-doors with the freedom of out-doors" (1), a pleasant spot where he takes his ease and his view of "Charlemagne," the name he has given to Mount Greylock. Although on several occasions he compares the piazza to a ship's deck that in winter reminds him of "weathering Cape Horn" (3), he more often evokes images of the theater, as he looks out over the picturesque scenery on all sides, or reading, as he alludes to the Renaissance authors whose company he enjoys on his porch. The name *piazza* seems eminently Hawthornean and explicitly literary, suggesting the author's solitude – heightened by his identification with the isolated Marianna – and preference for the world of art over reality.

If *Benito Cereno* is a piazza tale in this sense, it would seem intended to belong to a picturesque and privileged aesthetic. Certainly, it would not appear that Melville meant for it the kind of reading it has received since the mid-twentieth century – as a trenchant consideration of the most sensitive racial and political issues dividing America. The primary meaning of *piazza*, however, is a large, open marketplace or square. It is an Italian word deriving from Greek and Latin words for "broad street" or "courtyard." Its French cognate is *place*, its Spanish cognate *plaza*. It provides a wide open space for city dwellers of all classes to stroll, meet, do business, and mix with others. The October 1851 issue of *Harper's New Monthly Magazine* contains both an excerpt from *Moby-Dick* and an article titled "Lima and the Limanians," which provides striking visual images of the many classes and races that intermingle in the Plaza at the center of the city of Lima, Peru (Figures 3 and 4). At the end of *Benito Cereno*, the shocking details of Melville's description of the Plaza in Lima demonstrate a full awareness of Spain's violent colonial history in South America. There is no aesthetic detachment, no romantic or sentimental musing to which a viewer may retreat from the "real" story of human and national cruelty. In the Plaza in Lima, as Melville says in "The Piazza," "truth comes in with darkness," a darkness that Melville has identified with dark skins, dark deeds, and dark histories. It would be a mistake to assume that Melville's literary piazza provides a safe haven or a cozy retreat.

A piazza tale, then, might be thought of as a narrative that provides literary space for cultural conflict, makes its masked tensions visible, and allows them to play themselves out in a public arena. If we read *Benito Cereno* as a piazza tale in this sense, it becomes a story where multiple cultures, races, and points of view may display themselves in juxtaposition, if not in harmony with one another. As we see on the decks of the *San Dominick*,

COMING FROM MASS.

Figure 3. Coming from Mass. From "Lima and the Limanians." *Harper's New Monthly Magazine* (October 1851). *Courtesy of the Boston Public Library.*

PERUVIAN CAVALIER.

Figure 4 Peruvian Cavalier. From "Lima and the Limanians." *Courtesy of the Boston Public Library.*

a piazza tale may expose different races and classes to one another so that an outsider may wander freely among them, as Delano does. To understand Delano's point of view more fully, however, we need to see the piazza tale from the perspective of those whom he observes: the slaves.

EQUILIBRIUM IN THE SLAVE NARRATIVE

In rewriting Hawthorne's histories, Melville creates a broader vantage than the manse's parlor or farmhouse porch could provide. Whereas Hawthorne's historical landscape tends to be divided between opposite domains – the town and the wilderness – Melville's Plaza flattens such hierarchies and widens the space within which historical characters may move. *Benito Cereno* is not only history, however. It is also a slave narrative. It draws on the historical accounts of slave revolts – Amasa Delano's chapter in the *Narrative*, Thomas Grey's version of the Nat Turner rebellion

(1831), the newspaper accounts of the *Amistad* (1839) and *Creole* (1841) revolts – and also on some of the most popular and celebrated works of the 1840s and 1850s: Harriet Beecher Stowe's *Uncle Tom's Cabin* (1852) and Frederick Douglass's *Narrative* (1845) and "The Heroic Slave" (1851). As a slave narrative, *Benito Cereno* attempts to strike a balance between people divided by race and class, thus speaking to the new multiracial readership of popular works on slavery.

Until the late twentieth century, scholars thought that the main sources for Melville's treatment of a slave revolt were historical events rather than literary texts. Harold Scudder identified the real Amasa Delano in 1928, and Delano's *Narrative* provides a fascinating backdrop for *Benito Cereno*, especially in the evidence it supplies of how Melville heightened Delano's goodness and peaceableness and Cereno's helplessness. The historical Delano sued Benito Cereno for nonpayment of what Cereno owed him for repaired sails and demanded a half share of the confiscated ship and slaves. Cereno fought back vigorously, calling Delano a "monster." One of Delano's sailors, an ex-convict from Botany Bay, also used hostile language, calling him a "pirate," and the *Narrative* has traditionally been taken to show the flaws in Delano's character. Melville's Delano is a more ambiguous character, whose innocence and generosity may be seen as both positive and negative traits and whose nature seems of psychological and literary, as well as historical, interest.

The *Amistad* mutiny also has received considerable attention as a source for *Benito Cereno*, and indeed the stories are remarkably congruent (see Karcher, "Riddle"; Osagie; Sale). At the time of this incident, 1839, Spain had supposedly ceased its traffic in slaves, but traders still seized Africans and imported them to Cuba, gave them Spanish names to conceal their identities, and tried to assimilate them into the Cuban slave population. The *Amistad's* owners, Pedro Montez and Jose Ruiz, had just left Havana with a cargo of such slaves, when under the leadership of Joseph Cinque, or Sengbe Pieh, as he was known in Africa, they rose up and killed the captain and some of the crew, demanding that Montez steer a course for Africa (Figure 5). Montez complied by day but changed the course to a northerly direction by night, until the ship fetched up on the shores of Long Island. The case then went to court, where it became a cause célèbre for abolitionists and a political embarrassment for U.S. relations with Spain. In the end, John Quincy Adams, defending the slaves, argued that they had been illegally kidnapped and therefore did not belong to the Spanish owners and must be returned to Africa. Abolitionists rejoiced, and missionaries from the American Missionary Association rallied to raise funds and

Figure 5. Joseph Cinque. Painted by Nathaniel Jocelyn, ca. 1840. *Courtesy of the New Haven Colony Historical Society, New Haven, Connecticut.*

accompany the slaves back to Mende, in what is now Sierra Leone. In spite of the similarities between this incident and *Benito Cereno*, some of which can be traced directly to contemporary news accounts, they end quite differently, with the Mende slaves, or most of them, returning safely home.

Although the *Amistad* brought slave revolt to American shores, it was a Spanish ship and thus in some ways remote from the heart of American concerns, particularly among southern slaveholders, that a homegrown revolutionary, like Toussaint L'Ouverture in Haiti in the 1790s, might emerge. (Nat Turner almost earned that distinction in 1831 but could not mobilize his local revolt into a national movement.) The rebellion on the *Creole*, which took place shortly after the *Amistad*, in 1841, involved an American ship sailing from Virginia to New Orleans with a load of slaves (Figure 6). Their leader, Madison Washington, seized the ship and directed it to British-owned Nassau, where the slaves were acknowledged and allowed to disperse into the countryside — much to the anger and mortification of the United States. Coincidentally, the *Amistad* and *Creole* revolts took place shortly before and during Melville's seafaring years, when news of such happenings traveled rapidly through the maritime world and when his own cousin, Guert Gansevoort, witnessed and put down an incipient mutiny

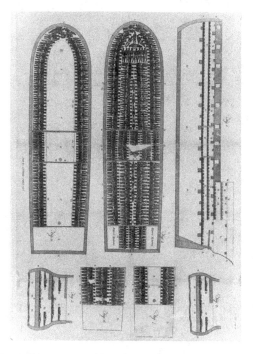

Figure 6. Cross-section of a slave ship. *Courtesy Boston Athenaeum.*

on the *Somers* in 1842 and Melville himself participated in a mutiny in Tahiti. Melville had plenty of material on which to draw for his account of revolt at sea.

Until quite recently, however, there has been little attention paid to the question of whether Melville could have read or adapted aspects of the more literary slave narratives of Stowe or Douglass. Part of this neglect can be attributed to lack of evidence. No copies of *Uncle Tom's Cabin* or Douglass's *Narrative* have emerged with Melville's marginal annotations, like his volumes of Dante's and Milton's works discovered not long ago by book dealers. A second problem is that scholars have tended not to look for evidence of Melville's reading of noncanonical works, especially those by women or nonwhite authors. Charlene Avallone, for example, has argued that scholars have ignored the clear evidence that Melville read Harriet Martineau's novel about slavery, *The Hour and the Man* (1840), although he wrote an appreciative letter about it to his neighbor Sarah Morewood. Sheila Post-Lauria has shown that Melville knew popular print culture

well and chose outlets for his stories according to how much they wel-
comed challenging material. *Putnam's* included many works on abolition
and social reform in its pages, and Melville sent them his most provocative
stories. Nevertheless, a persistent strain of Melville criticism has clung to
the notion that Melville did not write for or draw inspiration from the popular literary market, which was dominated by women writers and reform-
ers, including former slaves.

Recent research has changed that picture. Sarah Robbins has argued
persuasively that like Stowe, Melville responded with outrage to the passage
of the Fugitive Slave Act in 1850. Writing for the *National Era*, a popular
reformist venue, Stowe created a successful hybrid of traditional female genres – what Robbins calls the style of "domestic didactics" – and urgent political and social issues. In writing *Benito Cereno* for *Putnam's*, which had
already signaled in its articles and reviews a warmly appreciative response
to *Uncle Tom's Cabin*, Melville implicitly responded positively to that novel,
although in a very different register that might be identified with the masculine antisentimental styles *Putnam's* favored. Thus Melville's exposure of
Delano's sentimental notions of race, which could have been seen as directed
against Stowe, who expressed such views in characters like Augustine
St. Clare, might now be understood as doing something similar to Stowe, but
in a more masculine idiom. Internal evidence in Melville's story, as well as
the external historical conditions of the literary marketplace in which both
Melville and Stowe sought readers, suggests that Melville could not have
avoided knowing about or responding to Stowe's work.

The case for Melville's knowledge of Frederick Douglass also has
emerged in recent scholarship. Eric Sundquist has established the close
affinity between the two authors and the centrality of slavery as an issue
for classic American white authors, and other critics have noticed the par-
allels between them. Maggie Montesinos Sale draws attention to the
phrase "slumbering volcano," which Melville uses to describe the hidden
possibility of a slave revolt in *Benito Cereno* and which Douglass employed
in his speech of April 23, 1849: "the slaveholders are sleeping on slumbering volcanoes, if they did but know it" ("Volcano" 151). John Stauffer, in
The Black Hearts of Men, establishes that Douglass included references
to Melville's work, specifically *Moby-Dick*, in *Frederick Douglass' Paper*.
Following this lead, Robert K. Wallace has shown the close proximity between
the two authors in the late 1840s and early 1850s, from New Bedford,
Massachusetts, where both worked on the waterfront, to Albany, New York,
where Melville lived and Douglass lectured, to New York City, which Douglass
visited repeatedly while Melville was living there and haunting the same

neighborhoods where Douglass gave public speeches and garnered extensive public notice in the papers Melville read. In a coincidental tangent,
one of the issues of *Putnam's* in which *Benito Cereno* appeared also con-
tained an extremely positive review of Douglass's second autobiography,
My Bondage and My Freedom. The "Slumbering Volcano" speech included
a reference to the *Creole* mutiny, which Douglass later expanded into his
only fictional work, "The Heroic Slave," published several times between
1851 and 1853. Without evidence of a direct link between the two men,
Wallace shows convincingly that it would have been difficult for Melville
not to have encountered Douglass in person, in writing, or in the considerable news coverage that surrounded Douglass's visits to New York.

It's not that Stauffer's and Wallace's most remarkable finding, modestly phrased
in Wallace's book, is "that there was an anti-slavery and non-white audience for Melville's work" (53). This fact suggests that by the time Melville
wrote *Benito Cereno*, he was aware of having African American readers and
could conceivably have been writing for and to them, anticipating a response
in very different publications from the white-owned venues he had worked
in before. This fact makes *Benito Cereno* conceivably one of the first
American slave narratives to be written for two races.

It's not that *Uncle Tom's Cabin*, Frederick Douglass's *Narrative*, and
other writings did not have multiracial readers. They did. William Wells
Brown emulated *Uncle Tom's Cabin* in his own *Clotel* (1853), as did Harriet
Jacobs in her *Incidents in the Life of a Slave Girl* (1861). Stowe studied
Douglass's writings, as well as earlier slave narratives by Josiah Henson
(1849) and Henry Bibb (1849). Douglass reviewed *Uncle Tom's Cabin*, and
Martin Delany, author of *Blake; or, the Huts of America* (1861-1862), exco-
riated it. Among abolitionists, as Stauffer has shown, close bonds across
the color line created an enthusiastic audience for writings by both black
and white authors on slavery.

But both Stowe and Douglass lament the melancholy fact that their
real audience, the people they most need and want to influence, are mainstream white readers. When in the final chapter of *Uncle Tom's Cabin*, Stowe
rises to jeremiadic heights of eloquence, she speaks to the "generous,
noble-minded men and women of the South," the "farmers of Massachusetts,
of New Hampshire, of Vermont, of Connecticut," and the "mothers of
America," who can influence the "sons of the free states" to abolish slavery
(622-24) – in other words, the white readers who buy her books. Although
she addresses mothers and fathers throughout the novel, it is clear that
she does not include slave mothers and fathers in those appeals. Whatever
Stowe might have expected in the way of African American readers, her

novel shows that the ones she would most like to help could not read the book themselves. Douglass records a similar dilemma in his *Narrative*, when he remembers that he is outside the circle of slave culture and can no longer sing its songs or participate in its rituals. The isolation he experiences on escaping north is heightened by the fact that none of his former comrades can buy or read the poignant words he has written. Indeed, Douglass suggests throughout the book that he is in effect mute, until the dramatic moment in Nantucket when he is called upon to speak and, in the final words of the book, knows himself and speaks his heart: "I felt myself a slave" (326). Ironically, at this moment of free utterance, Douglass can communicate that paradoxical truth only to whites.

In terms of an *intended* audience, then, Stowe's and Douglass's early slave narratives appear to be directed primarily at white readers. In this sense, they are devious and unbalanced. While seeking to liberate the enchained slave, they must speak through and around, but not *to*, him or her. By contrast, Melville may have been writing to and for black readers, even if they were not slaves but, as was more likely, members of an educated northern middle class. If so, his story establishes an equilibrium between the different audiences for his narrative, or at least more of a balance than Stowe or Douglass might have imagined in their first antislavery works. That balance maintains a subtle racial tension throughout the story that lends resonance to its mysterious plot and characters.

PERFORMANCE, MELODRAMA, AND THE TABLEAU

Benito Cereno bears a strong resemblance to such literary genres as the historical tale and the slave narrative. But at certain points, the story departs from written sources and launches into a theatrical performance that depends not on words but on acting. A considerable portion of the story's events are staged as scenes of few words: Delano's encounter with the sailor with the knot, his wordless exchange with the sailor carrying a hidden jewel, Babo's and Cereno's offstage conferences, Atufal's appearances in heavily symbolic chains before Cereno, the hatchet-polishers' silent signals to the multitude streaming below them on deck, the "slumbering negress" and her seemingly natural sexuality and show of maternal love. The context for these theatrical productions includes two kinds of performance: African song and dance and American melodrama, especially the tableau.

Sterling Stuckey has established how much Melville owes to African performance traditions in a number of his works, including *Moby-Dick* and especially in relation to the Ring Shout and Pip's tambourine music in the chapter titled "Midnight, Forecastle" ("Tambourine"). Stuckey's extended reading of *Benito Cereno* reveals the importance of the women's chanting, the percussion of the hatchet-polishers, and the "droning and druling" of the oakum-pickers' bagpipe-like music in creating meaningful nonverbal communication among the Africans (*Storm*). This blend of sounds distracts Delano from the Spanish sailors' attempts to communicate with him, heartens the slaves as they struggle to keep their composure throughout their ordeal, and steels them for battle when the decisive moment comes. What Delano simply dismisses as background noise knits the slaves together into a community, preserving their cultural identity in the face of white oppression. As Cereno affirms in the deposition, the women "sang songs and danced – not gaily, but solemnly; and before the engagement with the boats, as well as during the action, they sang melancholy songs to the negroes, and ... this melancholy tone was more inflaming than a different one would have been, and was so intended" (102) [in this edition]. These songs are forcefully reminiscent of the songs Douglass records in his *Narrative* as "revealing at once the highest joy and the deepest sadness. . . . This they would sing, as a chorus, to words which to many would seem unmeaning jargon, but which, nevertheless, were full of meaning to themselves." The slaves' songs conveyed to Douglass "my first glimmering conception of the dehumanizing character of slavery. . . . The songs of the slave represent the sorrows of his heart; and he is relieved by them, only as an aching heart is relieved by its tears" (262-63). Whether Melville read Douglass's words or not, his description of the Africans' music reflects an awareness of its power to inspire strong emotion and effect serious action, even revolt.

Along with music, the scenes on the *San Dominick* show the deep majesty of African drama. As Iyunolu Folayan Osagie explains, "Drama or theater is prevalent in African cultural performance. Cultural performance, as employed here, embraces the participatory practice of African drama" (103). From the merest boy to the elders, from the warriors to the women and their babies, every African plays an active role in *Benito Cereno*. Furthermore, each understands the political significance of his or her participation. This is no mere "juggling play," as Delano calls the scene in the cuddy. Instead, as Osagie emphasizes, the "power of the theater" becomes "both a useful and a dangerous weapon in the hands of the masses" (103). According to Joy Morrison, African theater exists not just for entertainment but "because it is part of the whole fabric of African life and culture, existing as part of the larger communication environment which includes dance, drama, storytelling, music, games, and visual arts" (qtd. in Osagie 104).

One of the greatest mistakes a non-African reader might make is assuming that the masters succeed in silencing the slaves. The story shows how the "communication environment" of dance, song, and acting sustains them throughout their ordeal, something that European and American observers cannot fathom.

Another theatrical context is that of popular melodrama. Melville attended performances of Douglas Jerrold's nautical melodramas in London and many forms of popular entertainment in New York. He lived in a period when melodrama was moving from its late-eighteenth-century revolutionary phase, as a form of popular and political drama for classes excluded from the court-sponsored comedies and tragedies, to becoming a source of mainstream pleasure. Peter Brooks and David Grimsted have shown the powerful influence of melodrama on European and American culture, especially in democratizing the theater and providing a site of resistance against cultural elites and authorities. Melodrama's aesthetic of emotional excess, strong action, simple moral conflicts, and exaggerated physical gestures often proved offensive to conservative tastes, but it also offered liberating and subversive enactments of popular impulses and desires.

Benito Cereno, of course, might be the last of Melville's works one would think of as melodramatic, with its solemn and weighty issues and conflicts. Nevertheless, as Brooks's analysis allows us to see, melodrama uses several strategies that Melville also found effective. One is what Brooks calls the "text of muteness" (56). Many eighteenth-century European melodramas included nonspeaking characters, partly because the form emphasized music, mime, and action over words, but also because the mute character could express powerful meanings through gesture. The language of the body can say things that words cannot, and such a language is particularly compelling as embodied in the politically dispossessed, especially women, children, and servants. The emblematic figure of muteness in *Benito Cereno* is Atufal, of whom Babo says, "How like a mute Atufal moves." Babo's statement reminds us that Atufal is only pretending to be mute – he is *like* a mute – but for the purposes of the scene of excessive punishment, he *is* a mute, a figure of heroic, uncompromising silence, whose resistance represents the unspeakableness of the slaves' story. Such principled muteness gives a new reading to the idea that speech defines identity: Douglass is not a man until he speaks at the end of his *Narrative*. Freedom to withhold speech figures as largely in *Benito Cereno* as does freedom of speech, and thus the other unspeaking characters, such as the "slumbering negress" and most of the other slaves, can be seen as principled resisters too.

The other strategy that Melville may have adopted from melodrama is the tableau. As Brooks explains, "There tends throughout melodramas, and most especially at the ends of scenes or acts, to be a resolution of meaning in *tableau,* where the characters' attitudes and gestures, compositionally arranged and frozen for a moment, give, like the illustrative painting, a visual summary of the emotional situation" (48). The tableau provides a moment of intense awareness, a space for strong emotion, and a meaning that escapes language and depends on sensation. Using a typology of gestures, it arouses automatic rather than considered responses and suggests that humans everywhere are the same underneath their social masks and protective skins. By exaggerating experience and representing it visually, the tableau stops action. It asks the audience, in Stowe's famous phrase, to "feel right" (624) and lends full credence to that mode of understanding and communication.

In *Benito Cereno,* Melville includes a number of moments of tableau that show the different dramatic strains we have been considering here. One appears in the midst of Delano's visit:

> The casks were being hoisted in, when some of the eager
> negroes accidentally jostled Captain Delano, where he stood by
> the gangway; so that, unmindful of Don Benito, yielding to the
> impulse of the moment, with good-natured authority he bade the
> blacks stand back; to enforce his words making use of a half-
> mirthful, half-menacing gesture. Instantly the blacks paused,
> just where they were, each negro and negress suspended in his
> or her posture, exactly as the word had found them – for a few
> seconds continuing so – while, as between the responsive posts
> of a telegraph, an unknown syllable ran from man to man among
> the perched oakum-pickers. While the visitor's attention was
> fixed by this scene, suddenly the hatchet-polishers half rose, and
> a rapid cry came from Don Benito. (69)

As the scene begins, Delano is characteristically asserting his authority, using the language of thinly veiled impatience: "with good-natured authority he bade the blacks stand back." Recognizing that his words may not be fully effective by themselves, or perhaps unconscious of his actions, he also resorts to physical signs: "to enforce his words making use of a half-mirthful, half-menacing gesture." Unwittingly, though, he conveys a message that his words did not intend, for "instantly the blacks paused, just where they were, each negro and negress suspended in his or her posture, exactly as the word had found them." In their "suspended" postures,

the blacks express fully their displeasure and their awareness that restraint
is nevertheless the preferable policy. Their gestures and attitudes convey
their feelings perfectly, and no more communication is necessary. Nevertheless, "as between the responsive posts of a telegraph, an unknown syllable
ran from man to man among the perched oakum-pickers." This "syllable,"
which Delano cannot understand, conveys a decision and a policy that the
oakum-pickers then adopt, moving among the blacks "with gestures friendly
and familiar, almost jocose, bidding [each person], in substance, not to be
a fool." The tableau ends in an action that interprets the gestures, resolves
the tension, and restores order. But it has also been tremendously powerful in telling a story the slaves will not tell in words, and it has shown that
words are not necessary. This "flash" of insight suggests that the Africans'
performance is supple and effective as a form of communication, pro-
ductive of political agency, and deeply terrifying as well, for when "the
hatchet-polishers half rose," Cereno instantly recognizes the implied threat:
"a rapid cry came from Don Benito."

BENITO CERENO AND ITS AUDIENCES

Melville's reworkings of literary texts and performance strategies deepen
and complicate his narrative. They help explain why it captured the attention of his contemporaries. The story of how it continues to have meaning
today takes up Melville's changing critical reception in the century and a
half since *Benito Cereno*'s publication.

The question of *Benito Cereno*'s meaning has received sustained attention in its long critical history. Some scholars have argued that Melville's
portrayal of Babo as African savage shows his racism (Kaplan). Others
have suggested that Melville's proximity to Judge Lemuel Shaw, his father-
in-law and the chief justice of the Massachusetts Supreme Court, muted
Melville's criticism of the laws protecting slavery (Robertson-Lorant).
Some have seen Melville as a misunderstood rebel, who, after the commer-
cial failure of his ambitious novels *Moby-Dick* (1851) and *Pierre* (1852),
chose a more constrained form, the short story, and a more ironic, compressed style as a way of subverting complacent readers with truths that
the superficial skimmers of his pages would not comprehend (Fisher;
Dillingham). Others have suggested that Melville did not isolate or alien-
ate himself from his readers but in fact selected the social issues that he
knew would find appreciative readers among the subscribers to popular
magazines such as *Putnam's* and *Harper's* (Post-Lauria). Melville has been
seen as complicit in American exploitation of racial and social outsiders

(Dimock), as protesting against political authority (Rogin) and literary tradition (Reynolds), and as moving within and expressing the conflicting discourses of his cultural and political milieu (Lee; Levine; Nelson; Castronovo; Sundquist; Kelley). He has appeared as heroically resisting the strictures of a racist society (Bryant) and as tragically failing where other, more marginalized authors took greater risks (Karcher, "Riddle"). Few would disagree, though, that the story continues to excite controversy and to raise profound questions about the central crisis of nineteenth-century American culture – slavery and its threat to the union of North and South – and about the multiple existential and political issues rising from that crisis and extending into our own time.

More troubling to readers, perhaps, is the question of what *Benito Cereno* meant to Melville himself. Much current criticism has been directed at recovering Melville's historical context and identifying the allusions that escape a twenty-first-century reader but resonated with Melville and his nineteenth-century audience. For example, the image of the ship as a "monastery" filled with "dark moving figures . . . as of Black Friars pacing the cloisters" and its name, the *San Dominick*, might alert the historically minded reader to the fact that the Dominican movement arose in medieval Spain, along with the Inquisition, which, in its efforts at cleansing the Catholic Church, tortured Jews and Moors, leading to their eventual expulsion from Spain. The references to Castile and León and to the Spanish flag might remind one that Ferdinand and Isabella joined their separate kingdoms to create a more perfect Union (a concept subject to ferocious debate in mid-nineteenth-century America), one that sent Christopher Columbus to the New World and extended its sway over land and sea, using the Inquisition to establish its control. The allusion to Charles V of Spain, to whom Cereno is compared, recalls the emperor who brought Spain into the African slave trade, not long after the Dominican priest Bartolomé de Las Casas advised Columbus to import African slaves to Hispaniola rather than to impress the native workforce. The reader might further note the implied reference to Santo Domingo, where, at the time when the story supposedly takes place (1799; Melville changed the date of Amasa Delano's actual encounter with Benito Cereno in 1805 to the earlier date), Toussaint L'Ouverture was leading the revolt that resulted in freedom for blacks in what became Haiti. Allusions to Guy Fawkes and James I of England also evoke potent images of conspiracy and revolt. These details and many others point to a history of global trade in slaves; political intrigue and revolution; religious and national efforts at empire building; and the use of torture, kidnapping, and warfare to subdue non-Europeans around the world – all surfacing at a time when Americans confronted the specter of slave uprisings at home. It seems clear that Melville's allusions evoke a vast network of historical and political forces converging on the slave trade as a global transhistorical phenomenon.

Like the other contexts we have considered for Melville's work, these patterns and associations may clarify the story's range of references without necessarily resolving its meanings. *Benito Cereno* is a rich and capacious text. Its greatest gift may be the opportunity it offers every reader to weigh this perplexing case according to its many possible frames of interpretation. In that sense, it invites readers to exercise their liberty – and their responsibility – to judge wisely.

WORKS CITED

References to Melville's works derive from the Northwestern-Newberry edition, listed below, and are abbreviated as follows:

MD   *Moby-Dick*
PT   *Piazza Tales*
Corr   *Correspondence*

Adler, Joyce. *War in Melville's Imagination.* New York: New York UP, 1981.
Altschuler, Glenn C. "Whose Foot on Whose Throat? A Re-examination of Melville's *Benito Cereno.*" *CLA Journal* 3 (Mar. 1975): 383-92.
Avallone, Charlene. "Harriet Martineau, Herman Melville, and the Romancing of Haitian History." Paper presented at Herman Melville and Frederick Douglass: A Sesquicentennial Celebration. New Bedford, June 2005.
Brooks, Peter. *The Melodramatic Imagination: Balzac, Henry James, Melodrama, and the Mode of Excess.* New Haven: Yale UP, 1976.
Bryant, John. "The Persistence of Melville: Representative Writer for a Multicultural Age." *Melville's Ever-Moving Dawn: Centennial Essays.* Ed. John Bryant and Robert Milder. Kent: Kent State UP, 1997.
Burkholder, Robert E., ed. *Critical Essays on Herman Melville's 'Benito Cereno.'* New York: G. K. Hall, 1992.
Castronovo, Russ. *Fathering the Nation: American Genealogies of Slavery and Freedom.* Berkeley: U of California P, 1995.
Delano, Amasa. *Delano's Voyages of Commerce and Discovery: Amasa Delano in China, the Pacific Islands, Australia, and South America, 1789-1807.* Ed. Eleanor Roosevelt Seagraves. Stockbridge: Berkshire House, 1994.
Delbanco, Andrew. *Melville: His World and Work.* New York: Knopf, 2005.
Dillingham, William. *Melville's Short Fiction, 1853-1856.* Athens: U of Georgia P, 1977.
Dimock, Wai-chee. *Empire for Liberty: Melville and the Poetics of Individualism.* Princeton: Princeton UP, 1989.

Douglass, Frederick. "The Heroic Slave." *Autographs for Freedom*. Ed. Julia Griffiths. Cleveland: John P. Jewett, 1853. 174-239.

——. *Narrative of the Life of Frederick Douglass, an American Slave*. 1845. *The Classic Slave Narratives*. Ed. Henry Louis Gates. New York: Penguin, 1987.

——. "Slavery, the Slumbering Volcano: An Address Delivered in New York, New York, on 23 April 1849." *The Frederick Douglass Papers, Series One: Speeches, Debates, and Interviews*. 5 vols. Ed. John W. Blassingame. New Haven: Yale UP, 1979-1992. 2: 148-159.

Fisher, Marvin. *Going Under: Melville's Short Fiction and the American 1850s*. Baton Rouge: Louisiana State UP, 1977.

Fredericks, Nancy. *Melville's Art of Democracy*. Athens: U of Georgia P, 1995.

Grimsted, David. *Melodrama Unveiled: American Theater and Culture, 1800-1850*. Chicago: U of Chicago P, 1968.

Hughes, Henry. "Amasa Delano and the Dialogics of Honesty." Paper presented at Herman Melville and Frederick Douglass: A Sesquicentennial Celebration. New Bedford, June 2005.

Kaplan, Sidney. "Herman Melville and the American National Sin: The Meaning of 'Benito Cereno.'" *Journal of Negro History* 41 (Oct. 1956): 311-38; 42 (Jan. 1957): 11-37.

Karcher, Carolyn L. "The Moderate and the Radical: Melville and Child on the Civil War and Reconstruction." *ESQ: A Journal of the American Renaissance* 45.3-4 (1999): 187-257.

——. "The Riddle of the Sphinx: Melville's 'Benito Cereno' and the *Amistad* Case." *Critical Essays on Herman Melville's 'Benito Cereno.'* Ed. Robert E. Burkholder. New York: G. K. Hall, 1992.

——. *Shadow over the Promised Land: Slavery, Race, and Violence in Melville's America*. Baton Rouge: Louisiana State UP, 1980.

Kavanagh, James H. "That Hive of Subtlety: 'Benito Cereno' and the Liberal Hero." *Ideology and Classic American Literature*. Ed. Sacvan Bercovitch and Myra Jehlen. Cambridge: Cambridge UP, 1986.

Kelley, Wyn. "The Style of Lima: Colonialism, Urban Form, and 'The Town-Ho's Story.'" *Melville "Among the Nations."* Ed. Sanford E. Marovitz and A. C. Christodoulou. Kent: Kent State UP, 2001.

Lee, Maurice S. "Melville's Subversive Political Philosophy: 'Benito Cereno' and the Fate of Speech." *American Literature* 72.3 (2000): 495-519.

Leslie, Joshua, and Sterling Stuckey. "The Death of Benito Cereno: A Reading of Herman Melville on Slavery." *Journal of Negro History* 67 (1982): 287-301.

Levine, Robert S., ed. *The Cambridge Companion to Melville*. Cambridge: Cambridge UP, 1998.

——. *Conspiracy and Romance: Studies in Brockden Brown, Cooper, Hawthorne, and Melville*. Cambridge: Cambridge UP, 1989.

——. *Martin Delany, Frederick Douglass, and the Politics of Representative Identity*. Chapel Hill: U of North Carolina P, 1997.

——. "Teaching in the Multiracial Classroom: Reconsidering 'Benito Cereno.'" *Teaching What You're Not: Identity Politics in Higher Education.* Ed. Katherine J. Mayberry. New York: New York UP, 1996.

"Lima and the Limanians." *Harper's New Monthly Magazine* Oct. 1851: 598-610.

Melville, Herman. *Correspondence.* Ed. Lynn Horth. Vol. 14 of *The Writings of Herman Melville.* Ed. Harrison Hayford, Hershel Parker, and G. Thomas Tanselle. Evanston and Chicago: Northwestern UP and Newberry Library, 1993.

——. *Moby-Dick; or, the Whale.* Vol. 6 of *The Writings of Herman Melville.* Ed. Harrison Hayford, Hershel Parker, and G. Thomas Tanselle. Evanston and Chicago: Northwestern UP and the Newberry Library, 1988.

——. *The Piazza Tales and Other Prose Pieces, 1839-1860.* Ed. Harrison Hayford, Alma A. McDougall, and G. Thomas Tanselle. Vol. 9 of *The Writings of Herman Melville.* Ed. Harrison Hayford, Hershel Parker, and G. Thomas Tanselle. Evanston and Chicago: Northwestern UP and Newberry Library, 1987.

Morrison, Toni. "Unspeakable Things Unspoken: The Afro American Presence in American Literature." *Michigan Quarterly Review* 28 (1989): 1-34.

Nelson, Dana D. *The Word in Black and White: Reading "Race" in American Literature, 1638-1867.* New York: Oxford UP, 1992.

Osagie, Iyunolu Folayan. *The Amistad Revolt.* Athens: U of Georgia P, 2000.

Parker, Hershel. *Herman Melville: A Biography.* Vol. 1, 1819-1851. Baltimore and London: Johns Hopkins UP, 1996. Vol. II, 1851-1891. Baltimore and London: Johns Hopkins UP, 2002.

Post-Lauria, Sheila. *Correspondent Colorings: Melville in the Marketplace.* Amherst: U of Massachusetts P, 1996.

Reynolds, David. *Beneath the American Renaissance: The Subversive Imagination in the Age of Emerson and Melville.* New York: Knopf, 1988.

Robbins, Sarah. "Gendering the History of the Antislavery Narrative: Juxtaposing *Uncle Tom's Cabin* and *Benito Cereno, Beloved* and *Middle Passage.*" *American Quarterly* 49.3 (1997): 531-73.

Robertson-Lorant, Laurie. *Melville: A Biography.* New York: Clarkson Potter, 1996.

Rogin, Michael Paul. *Subversive Genealogy: The Politics and Art of Herman Melville.* New York: Knopf, 1983.

Sale, Maggie Montesinos. *The Slumbering Volcano: American Slave Ship Revolts and the Production of Rebellious Masculinity.* Durham: Duke UP, 1997.

Scudder, Harold H. "Melville's 'Benito Cereno' and Captain Delano's Voyages." *PMLA* 43 (1928): 502-32.

Stauffer, John. *The Black Hearts of Men: Radical Abolitionists and the Transformation of Race.* Cambridge: Harvard UP, 2002.

Stowe, Harriet Beecher. *Uncle Tom's Cabin; or, Life among the Lowly.* 1852. Ed. Ann Douglas. New York: Penguin, 1981.

Stuckey, Sterling. *Going through the Storm: The Influence of African American Art in History.* New York: Oxford UP, 1994.

——. "The Tambourine in Glory: African Culture and Melville's Art." *The Cambridge Companion to Herman Melville*. Ed. Robert S. Levine. Cambridge: Cambridge UP, 1998.

Sundquist, Eric J. "*Benito Cereno* and New World Slavery." *Critical Essays on Herman Melville's "Benito Cereno."* Ed. Robert E. Burkholder. New York: G. K. Hall, 1992.

——. "Slavery, Revolution, and the American Renaissance." *The American Renaissance Reconsidered*. Ed. Walter Benn Michaels and Donald E. Pease. Baltimore: Johns Hopkins UP, 1985.

——. *To Wake the Nations: Race in the Making of American Literature*. Cambridge: Belknap Press of Harvard UP, 1993.

Thomas, Brook. "The Legal Fictions of Herman Melville and Lemuel Shaw. *Critical Essays on Herman Melville's 'Benito Cereno.'* Ed. Robert E. Burkholder. New York: G. K. Hall, 1992.

Wallace, Robert K. *Douglass and Melville: Anchored Together in Neighborly Style*. New Bedford: Spinner, 2005.

Yellin, Jean Fagan. "Black Masks: Melville's 'Benito Cereno.'" *American Quarterly* 22 (Fall 1970): 678-89.

Benito Cereno

Herman Melville

Benito Cereno

I̲N̲ ̲T̲H̲E̲ ̲Y̲E̲A̲R̲ ̲1̲7̲9̲9̲,[1] Captain A̲m̲a̲s̲a̲ ̲D̲e̲l̲a̲n̲o̲, of Duxbury, in Massachusetts, commanding a large sealer and general trader, lay at anchor, with a valuable cargo, in the harbor of St. Maria – a small, desert, uninhabited island toward the southern extremity of the long coast of Chili. There he had touched for water.

On the second day, not long after dawn, while lying in his berth, his mate came below, informing him that a strange sail was coming into the bay. Ships were then not so plenty in those waters as now. He rose, dressed, and went on deck.

The morning was one peculiar to that coast. Everything was mute and calm; everything gray. The sea, though undulated into long roods

---

1. *1799:* Melville changed a number of details in his source, Amasa Delano's *Narrative,* including the date of the encounter (from 1805 to 1799) and the names of the ships: Delano's *Perseverence* to the *Bachelor's Delight* and Cereno's *Tryal* to the *San Dominick.*

of swells, seemed fixed, and was sleeked at the surface like waved lead that has cooled and set in the smelter's mould. The sky seemed a gray surtout.[2] Flights of troubled gray fowl, kith and kin with flights of troubled gray vapors among which they were mixed, skimmed low and fitfully over the waters, as swallows over meadows before storms. Shadows present, fore-shadowing deeper shadows to come.

To Captain Delano's surprise, the stranger, viewed through the glass, showed no colors; though to do so upon entering a haven, however uninhab-ited in its shores, where but a single other ship might be lying, was the cus-tom among peaceful seamen of all nations. Considering the lawlessness and loneliness of the spot, and the sort of stories, at that day, associated with those seas, Captain Delano's surprise might have deepened into some uneasiness had he not been a person of a singularly undistrustful good nature, not liable, except on extraordinary and repeated incentives, and hardly then, to indulge in personal alarms, any way involving the imputation of malign evil in man. Whether, in view of what humanity is capable, such a trait implies, along with a benevolent heart, more than ordinary quickness and accuracy of intellectual perception, may be left to the wise to determine.

But whatever misgivings might have obtruded on first seeing the stranger, would almost, in any seaman's mind, have been dissipated by observ-ing that, the ship, in navigating into the harbor, was drawing too near the land, for her own safety's sake, owing to a sunken reef making out off her bow. This seemed to prove her a stranger, indeed, not only to the sealer, but the island; consequently, she could be no wonted freebooter on that ocean. With no small interest, Captain Delano continued to watch her – a proceeding not much facilitated by the vapors partly mantling the hull, through which the far matin[3] light from her cabin streamed equivocally enough; much like the sun – by this time hemisphered on the rim of the horizon, and apparently, in com-pany with the strange ship, entering the harbor – which, wimpled by the same low, creeping clouds, showed not unlike a Lima intriguante's one sinister eye peering across the Plaza from the Indian loop-hole of her dusk *saya-y-manta.*[4]

It might have been but a deception of the vapors, but, the longer the stranger was watched, the more singular appeared her maneuvers. Ere long

---

2. *surtout:* Overcoat.
3. *matin:* Taking place in the morning. In the Christian church, the *matins* are the first wor-ship service of the day.
4. *saya-y-manta:* A veil worn by nineteenth-century Peruvian women in public. Concealing all of the face except one eye, it allows a woman to carry on her intrigues – "not unlike a Lima intriguante" – without discovery. (See Figure 3.)

it seemed hard to decide whether she meant to come in or no – what she wanted, or what she was about. The wind, which had breezed up a little during the night, was now extremely light and baffling, which the more increased the apparent uncertainty of her movements.

Surmising, at last, that it might be a ship in distress, Captain Delano ordered his whale-boat to be dropped, and, much to the wary opposition of his mate, prepared to board her, and, at the least, pilot her in. On the night previous, a fishing-party of the seamen had gone a long distance to some detached rocks out of sight from the sealer, and, an hour or two before day-break, had returned, having met with no small success. Presuming that the stranger might have been long off soundings, the good captain put sev-eral baskets of the fish, for presents, into his boat, and so pulled away. From her continuing too near the sunken reef, deeming her in danger, call-ing to his men, he made all haste to apprise those on board of their situa-tion. But, some time ere the boat came up, the wind, light though it was, having shifted, had headed the vessel off, as well as partly broken the vapors from about her.

Upon gaining a less remote view, the ship, when made signally visible on the verge of the leaden-hued swells, with the shreds of fog here and there raggedly furring her, appeared like a white-washed monastery after a thunder-storm, seen perched upon some dun cliff among the Pyrenees. But it was no purely fanciful resemblance which now, for a moment, almost led Captain Delano to think that nothing less than a ship-load of monks was before him. Peering over the bulwarks were what really seemed, in the hazy distance, throngs of dark cowls; while, fitfully revealed through the open port-holes, other dark moving figures were dimly descried, as of Black Friars[5] pacing the cloisters.

Upon a still nigher approach, this appearance was modified, and the true character of the vessel was plain – a Spanish merchantman of the first class; carrying negro slaves, amongst other valuable freight, from one colonial port to another. A very large, and, in its time, a very fine vessel, such as in those days were at intervals encountered along that main; some-times superseded Acapulco treasure-ships, or retired frigates of the Spanish king's navy, which, like superannuated Italian palaces, still, under a decline of masters, preserved signs of former state.

As the whale-boat drew more and more nigh, the cause of the peculiar pipe-clayed aspect of the stranger was seen in the slovenly neglect pervading

5. *Black Friars*: Members of the Dominican order of monks.

her. The spars, ropes, and great part of the bulwarks, looked woolly, from long unacquaintance with the scraper, tar, and the brush. Her keel seemed laid, her ribs put together, and she launched, from Ezekiel's Valley of Dry Bones.

In the present business in which she was engaged, the ship's general model and rig appeared to have undergone no material change from their original war-like and Froissart pattern. However, no guns were seen.

The tops were large, and were railed about with what had once been octagonal net-work, all now in sad disrepair. These tops hung overhead like three ruinous aviaries, in one of which was seen perched, on a ratlin, a white noddy, a strange fowl, so called from its lethargic, somnambulistic character, being frequently caught by hand at sea. Battered and mouldy, the castellated forecastle seemed some ancient turret, long ago taken by assault, and then left to decay. Toward the stern, two high-raised quarter galleries – the balustrades here and there covered with dry, tindery sea-moss – opening out from the unoccupied state-cabin, whose dead lights, for all the mild weather, were hermetically closed and calked – these tenantless balconies hung over the sea as if it were the grand Venetian canal. But the principal relic of faded grandeur was the ample oval of the shield-like sternpiece, intricately carved with the arms of Castile and Leon, medallioned about by groups of mythological or symbolical devices; uppermost and central of which was a dark satyr in a mask, holding his foot on the prostrate neck of a writhing figure, likewise masked.

Whether the ship had a figure-head, or only a plain beak, was not quite certain, owing to canvas wrapped about that part, either to protect it while undergoing a re-furbishing, or else decently to hide its decay. Rudely painted or chalked, as in a sailor freak, along the forward side of a sort of pedestal below the canvas, was the sentence, "*Seguid vuestro jefe,*" (follow your leader); while upon the tarnished head-boards, near by, appeared, in stately capitals, once gilt, the ship's name, "SAN DOMINICK,"[6] each letter streakingly corroded with tricklings of copper-spike rust; while, like mourning weeds, dark festoons of sea-grass slimily swept to and fro over the name, with every hearse-like roll of the hull.

As at last the boat was hooked from the bow along toward the gangway amidship, its keel, while yet some inches separated from the hull, harshly grated as on a sunken coral reef. It proved a huge bunch of conglobated barnacles adhering below the water to the side like a wen; a token of baffling airs and long calms passed somewhere in those seas.

---

6. *San Dominick:* The name recalls the earlier reference to Dominican friars, as well as European (French and Spanish) New World colonialism in the Caribbean.

Climbing the side, the visitor was at once surrounded by a clamorous throng of whites and blacks, but the latter outnumbering the former more than could have been expected, negro transportation-ship as the stranger in port was. But, in one language, and as with one voice, all poured out a common tale of suffering; in which the negresses, of whom there were not a few, exceeded the others in their dolorous vehemence. The scurvy, together with a fever, had swept off a great part of their number, more especially the Spaniards. Off Cape Horn, they had narrowly escaped shipwreck; then, for days together, they had lain tranced without wind; their provisions were low; their water next to none; their lips that moment were baked.

While Captain Delano was thus made the mark of all eager tongues, his one eager glance took in all the faces, with every other object about him.

Always upon first boarding a large and populous ship at sea, especially a foreign one, with a nondescript crew such as Lascars or Manilla men, the impression varies in a peculiar way from that produced by first entering a strange house with strange inmates in a strange land. Both house and ship, the one by its walls and blinds, the other by its high bulwarks like ramparts, hoard from view their interiors till the last moment; but in the case of the ship there is this addition; that the living spectacle it contains, upon its sudden and complete disclosure, has, in contrast with the blank ocean which zones it, something of the effect of enchantment. The ship seems unreal; these strange costumes, gestures, and faces, but a shadowy tableau just emerged from the deep, which directly must receive back what it gave.

Perhaps it was some such influence as above is attempted to be described, which, in Captain Delano's mind, heightened whatever, upon a staid scrutiny, might have seemed unusual; especially the conspicuous figures of four elderly grizzled negroes, their heads like black, doddered willow tops, who, in venerable contrast to the tumult below them, were couched sphynx-like, one on the starboard cat-head, another on the larboard, and the remaining pair face to face on the opposite bulwarks above the mainchains. They each had bits of unstranded old junk in their hands, and, with a sort of stoical self-content, were picking the junk into oakum,[7] a small heap of which lay by their sides. They accompanied the task with a continuous, low, monotonous chant; droning and druling away like so many grayheaded bag-pipers playing a funeral march.

---

7. *doddered*: Having lost the top branches, thus looking like a tree stump. *Junk*: An old piece of discarded rope. *Oakum*: Fibers taken or picked from twisted strands of old rope, then rewoven or used for joints and caulking.

The quarter-deck rose into an ample elevated poop, upon the forward verge of which, lifted, like the oakum-pickers, some eight feet above the general throng, sat along in a row, separated by regular spaces, the cross-legged figures of six other blacks; each with a rusty hatchet in his hand, which, with a bit of brick and a rag, he was engaged like a scullion in scouring; while between each two was a small stack of hatchets, their rusted edges turned forward awaiting a like operation. Though occasionally the four oakum-pickers would briefly address some person or persons in the crowd below, yet the six hatchet-polishers neither spoke to others, nor breathed a whisper among themselves, but sat intent upon their task, except at intervals, when, with the peculiar love in negroes of uniting industry with pastime, two and two they sideways clashed their hatchets together, like cymbals, with a barbarous din. All six, unlike the generality, had the raw aspect of unsophisticated Africans.

But that first comprehensive glance which took in those ten figures, with scores less conspicuous, rested but an instant upon them, as, impatient of the hubbub of voices, the visitor turned in quest of whomsoever it might be that commanded the ship.

But as if not unwilling to let nature make known her own case among his suffering charge, or else in despair of restraining it for the time, the Spanish captain, a gentlemanly, reserved-looking, and rather young man to a stranger's eye, dressed with singular richness, but bearing plain traces of recent sleepless cares and disquietudes, stood passively by, leaning against the main-mast, at one moment casting a dreary, spiritless look upon his excited people, at the next an unhappy glance toward his visitor. By his side stood a black of small stature, in whose rude face, as occasionally, like a shepherd's dog, he mutely turned it up into the Spaniard's, sorrow and affection were equally blended.

Struggling through the throng, the American advanced to the Spaniard, assuring him of his sympathies, and offering to render whatever assistance might be in his power. To which the Spaniard returned, for the present, but grave and ceremonious acknowledgments, his national formality dusked by the saturnine mood of ill health.

But losing no time in mere compliments, Captain Delano returning to the gangway, had his baskets of fish brought up; and as the wind still continued light, so that some hours at least must elapse ere the ship could be brought to the anchorage, he bade his men return to the sealer, and fetch back as much water as the whale-boat could carry, with whatever soft bread the steward might have, all the remaining pumpkins on board, with a box of sugar, and a dozen of his private bottles of cider.

Not many minutes after the boat's pushing off, to the vexation of all, the wind entirely died away, and the tide turning, began drifting back the ship helplessly seaward. But trusting this would not long last, Captain Delano sought with good hopes to cheer up the strangers, feeling no small satisfaction that, with persons in their condition he could – thanks to his frequent voyages along the Spanish main – converse with some freedom in their native tongue.

While left alone with them, he was not long in observing some things tending to heighten his first impressions; but surprise was lost in pity, both for the Spaniards and blacks, alike evidently reduced from scarcity of water and provisions; while long-continued suffering seemed to have brought out the less good-natured qualities of the negroes, besides, at the same time, impairing the Spaniard's authority over them. But, under the circumstances, precisely this condition of things was to have been anticipated. In armies, navies, cities, or families, in nature herself, nothing more relaxes good order than misery. Still, Captain Delano was not without the idea, that had Benito Cereno been a man of greater energy, misrule would hardly have come to the present pass. But the debility, constitutional or induced by the hardships, bodily and mental, of the Spanish captain, was too obvious to be overlooked. A prey to settled dejection, as if long mocked with hope he would not now indulge it, even when it had ceased to be a mock, the prospect of that day or evening at furthest, lying at anchor, with plenty of water for his people, and a brother captain to counsel and befriend, seemed in no perceptible degree to encourage him. His mind appeared unstrung, if not still more seriously affected. Shut up in these oaken walls, chained to one dull round of command, whose unconditionality cloyed him, like some hypochondriac abbot he moved slowly about, at times suddenly pausing, starting, or staring, biting his lip, biting his finger-nail, flushing, paling, twitching his beard, with other symptoms of an absent or moody mind. This distempered spirit was lodged, as before hinted, in as distempered a frame. He was rather tall, but seemed never to have been robust, and now with nervous suffering was almost worn to a skeleton. A tendency to some pulmonary complaint appeared to have been lately confirmed. His voice was like that of one with lungs half gone, hoarsely suppressed, a husky whisper. No wonder that, as in this state he tottered about, his private servant apprehensively followed him. Sometimes the negro gave his master his arm, or took his handkerchief out of his pocket for him; performing these and similar offices with that affectionate zeal which transmutes into something filial or fraternal acts in themselves but menial; and which has gained for the negro the repute of making the most pleasing

body servant in the world; one, too, whom a master need be on no stiffly
superior terms with, but may treat with familiar trust; less a servant than
a devoted companion.

Marking the noisy indocility of the blacks in general, as well as what
seemed the sullen inefficiency of the whites, it was not without humane satisfaction that Captain Delano witnessed the steady good conduct of Babo.

But the good conduct of Babo, hardly more than the ill-behavior of others, seemed to withdraw the half-lunatic Don Benito from his cloudy lan-
guor. Not that such precisely was the impression made by the Spaniard on
the mind of his visitor. The Spaniard's individual unrest was, for the present,
but noted as a conspicuous feature in the ship's general affliction. Still,
Captain Delano was not a little concerned at what he could not help taking
for the time to be Don Benito's unfriendly indifference towards himself. The
Spaniard's manner, too, conveyed a sort of sour and gloomy disdain, which
he seemed at no pains to disguise. But this the American in charity ascribed
to the harassing effects of sickness, since, in former instances, he had noted
that there are peculiar natures on whom prolonged physical suffering seems
to cancel every social instinct of kindness; as if forced to black bread themselves, they deemed it but equity that each person coming nigh them should,
indirectly, by some slight or affront, be made to partake of their fare.

But ere long Captain Delano bethought him that, indulgent as he was
at the first, in judging the Spaniard, he might not, after all, have exercised
charity enough. At bottom it was Don Benito's reserve which displeased
him; but the same reserve was shown towards all but his faithful personal
attendant. Even the formal reports which, according to sea-usage, were, at
stated times, made to him by some petty underling, either a white, mulatto
or black, he hardly had patience enough to listen to, without betraying con-
temptuous aversion. His manner upon such occasions was, in its degree,
not unlike that which might be supposed to have been his imperial countryman's, Charles V.,[8] just previous to the anchoritish retirement of that
monarch from the throne.

This splenetic disrelish of his place was evinced in almost every function pertaining to it. Proud as he was moody, he condescended to no personal mandate. Whatever special orders were necessary, their delivery was
delegated to his body-servant, who in turn transferred them to their ulti-
mate destination, through runners, alert Spanish boys or slave boys, like

---

8. *Charles V:* Born in 1500, he ruled as Charles I, king of Spain (1516–1556), and as Holy Roman
emperor (1519–1558). He spent the last two years of his life (1556–1558) in a monastery.

pages or pilot-fish within easy call continually hovering round Don Benito. So that to have beheld this undemonstrative invalid gliding about, apathetic and mute, no landsman could have dreamed that in him was lodged a dictatorship beyond which, while at sea, there was no earthly appeal.

Thus, the Spaniard, regarded in his reserve, seemed as the involuntary victim of mental disorder. But, in fact, his reserve might, in some degree, have proceeded from design. If so, then here was evinced the unhealthy climax of that icy though conscientious policy, more or less adopted by all commanders of large ships, which, except in signal emergencies, obliterates alike the manifestation of sway with every trace of sociality; transforming the man into a block, or rather into a loaded cannon, which, until there is call for thunder, has nothing to say. *trying so hard to justify*

Viewing him in this light, it seemed but a natural token of the perverse habit induced by a long course of such hard self-restraint, that, notwithstanding the present condition of his ship, the Spaniard should still persist in a demeanor, which, however harmless, or, it may be, appropriate, in a well appointed vessel, such as the San Dominick might have been at the outset of the voyage, was anything but judicious now. But the Spaniard perhaps thought that it was with captains as with gods: reserve, under all events, must still be their cue. But more probably this appearance of slumbering dominion might have been but an attempted disguise to conscious imbecility – not deep policy, but shallow device. But be all this as it might, whether Don Benito's manner was designed or not, the more Captain Delano noted its pervading reserve, the less he felt uneasiness at any particular manifestation of that reserve towards himself.

Neither were his thoughts taken up by the captain alone. Wonted to the quiet orderliness of the sealer's comfortable family of a crew, the noisy confusion of the San Dominick's suffering host repeatedly challenged his eye. Some prominent breaches not only of discipline but of decency were observed. These Captain Delano could not but ascribe, in the main, to the absence of those subordinate deck-officers to whom, along with higher duties, is entrusted what may be styled the police department of a populous ship. True, the old oakum-pickers appeared at times to act the part of monitorial constables to their countrymen, the blacks; but though occasionally succeeding in allaying trifling outbreaks now and then between man and man, they could do little or nothing toward establishing general quiet. The San Dominick was in the condition of a transatlantic emigrant ship, among whose multitude of living freight are some individuals, doubtless, as little troublesome as crates and bales; but the friendly remonstrances of such with their ruder companions are of not so much avail as the unfriendly arm of the mate. What the San Dominick wanted was, what the emigrant ship has, stern superior officers. But on these decks not so much as a fourth mate was to be seen.

The visitor's curiosity was roused to learn the particulars of those mishaps which had brought about such absenteeism, with its consequences; because, though deriving some inkling of the voyage from the wails which at the first moment had greeted him, yet of the details no clear understanding had been had. The best account would, doubtless, be given by the captain. Yet at first the visitor was loth to ask it, unwilling to provoke some distant rebuff. But plucking up courage, he at last accosted Don Benito, renewing the expression of his benevolent interest, adding, that did he (Captain Delano) but know the particulars of the ship's misfortunes, he would, perhaps, be better able in the end to relieve them. Would Don Benito favor him with the whole story?

Don Benito faltered; then, like some somnambulist suddenly interfered with, vacantly stared at his visitor, and ended by looking down on the deck. He maintained this posture so long, that Captain Delano, almost equally disconcerted, and involuntarily almost as rude, turned suddenly from him, walking forward to accost one of the Spanish seamen for the desired information. But he had hardly gone five paces, when with a sort of eagerness Don Benito invited him back, regretting his momentary absence of mind, and professing readiness to gratify him.

While most part of the story was being given, the two captains stood on the after part of the main-deck, a privileged spot, no one being near but the servant.

"It is now a hundred and ninety days," began the Spaniard, in his husky whisper, "that this ship, well officered and well manned, with several cabin passengers – some fifty Spaniards in all – sailed from Buenos Ayres bound to Lima, with a general cargo, hardware, Paraguay tea and the like – and," pointing forward, "that parcel of negroes, now not more than a hundred and fifty, as you see, but then numbering over three hundred souls. Off Cape Horn we had heavy gales. In one moment, by night, three of my best officers, with fifteen sailors, were lost, with the main-yard; the spar snapping under them in the slings, as they sought, with heavers, to beat down the icy sail. To lighten the hull, the heavier sacks of mate[9] were thrown into the sea, with most of the water-pipes lashed on deck at the time. And this last necessity it was, combined with the prolonged detentions

9. *mate*: Tea made from a South American shrub.

afterwards experienced, which eventually brought about our chief causes of suffering. When –"

Here there was a sudden fainting attack of his cough, brought on, no doubt, by his mental distress. His servant sustained him, and drawing a cordial from his pocket placed it to his lips. He a little revived. But unwilling to leave him unsupported while yet imperfectly restored, the black with one arm still encircled his master, at the same time keeping his eye fixed on his face, as if to watch for the first sign of complete restoration, or relapse, as the event might prove.

The Spaniard proceeded, but brokenly and obscurely, as one in a dream.

–"Oh, my God! rather than pass through what I have, with joy I would have hailed the most terrible gales; but –"

His cough returned and with increased violence; this subsiding, with reddened lips and closed eyes he fell heavily against his supporter.

"His mind wanders. He was thinking of the plague that followed the gales," plaintively sighed the servant; "my poor, poor master!" wringing one hand, and with the other wiping the mouth. "But be patient, Señor," again turning to Captain Delano, "these fits do not last long; master will soon be himself."

Don Benito reviving, went on; but as this portion of the story was very brokenly delivered, the substance only will here be set down.

It appeared that after the ship had been many days tossed in storms off the Cape, the scurvy broke out, carrying off numbers of the whites and blacks. When at last they had worked round into the Pacific, their spars and sails were so damaged, and so inadequately handled by the surviving mariners, most of whom were become invalids, that, unable to lay her northerly course by the wind, which was powerful, the unmanageable ship for successive days and nights was blown northwestward, where the breeze suddenly deserted her, in unknown waters, to sultry calms. The absence of the water-pipes now proved as fatal to life as before their presence had menaced it. Induced, or at least aggravated, by the more than scanty allowance of water, a malignant fever followed the scurvy; with the excessive heat of the lengthened calm, making such short work of it as to sweep away, as by billows, whole families of the Africans, and a yet larger number, proportionably, of the Spaniards, including, by a luckless fatality, every remaining officer on board. Consequently, in the smart west winds eventually following the calm, the already rent sails having to be simply dropped, not furled, at need, had been gradually reduced to the beggar's rags they were now. To procure substitutes for his lost sailors, as well as supplies of water and sails, the captain at the earliest opportunity had made for Baldivia [Valdivia], the southermost civilized port of Chili and South America; but upon nearing the coast the thick weather had prevented him from so much as sighting that harbor. Since which period, almost without a crew, and almost without canvas and almost without water, and at intervals giving its added dead to the sea, the San Dominick had been battledored about by contrary winds, inveigled by currents, or grown weedy in calms. Like a man lost in woods, more than once she had doubled upon her / own track.

"But throughout these calamities," huskily continued Don Benito, painfully turning in the half embrace of his servant, "I have to thank those negroes you see, who, though to your inexperienced eyes appearing unruly, have, indeed, conducted themselves with less of restlessness than even their owner could have thought possible under such circumstances."

Here he again fell faintly back. Again his mind wandered: but he rallied, and less obscurely proceeded.

"Yes, their owner was quite right in assuring me that no fetters would be needed with his blacks; so that while, as is wont in this transportation, those negroes have always remained upon deck – not thrust below, as in the Guinea-men – they have, also, from the beginning, been freely permitted to range within given bounds at their pleasure."

Once more the faintness returned – his mind roved – but, recovering, he resumed:

"But it is Babo here to whom, under God, I owe not only my own preservation, but likewise to him, chiefly, the merit is due, of pacifying his more ignorant brethren, when at intervals tempted to murmurings."

"Ah, master," sighed the black, bowing his face, "don't speak of me; Babo is nothing; what Babo has done was but duty."

"Faithful fellow!" cried Capt. Delano. "Don Benito, I envy you such a friend; slave I cannot call him."

As master and man stood before him, the black upholding the white, Captain Delano could not but bethink him of the beauty of that relationship which could present such a spectacle of fidelity on the one hand and confidence on the other. The scene was heightened by the contrast in dress, denoting their relative positions. The Spaniard wore a loose Chili jacket of dark velvet; white small clothes and stockings, with silver buckles at the knee and instep; a high-crowned sombrero, of fine grass; a slender sword, silver mounted, hung from a knot in his sash; the last being an almost invariable adjunct, more for utility than ornament, of a South American gentleman's dress to this hour. Excepting when his occasional nervous contortions brought about disarray, there was a certain precision in his attire, curiously at variance with the unsightly disorder around; especially in the belittered Ghetto,[10] forward of the main-mast, wholly occupied by the blacks.

The servant wore nothing but wide trowsers, apparently, from their coarseness and patches, made out of some old topsail; they were clean, and confined at the waist by a bit of unstranded rope, which, with his composed, deprecatory air at times, made him look something like a begging friar of St. Francis.[11]

However unsuitable for the time and place, at least in the blunt-thinking American's eyes, and however strangely surviving in the midst of all his afflictions, the toilette of Don Benito might not, in fashion at least, have gone beyond the style of the day among South Americans of his class. Though on the present voyage sailing from Buenos Ayres, he had avowed himself a native and resident of Chili, whose inhabitants had not so generally adopted the plain coat and once plebeian pantaloons; but, with a becoming modification, adhered to their provincial costume, picturesque as any in the world. Still, relatively to the pale history of the voyage, and his own pale face, there seemed something so incongruous in the Spaniard's apparel, as almost to suggest the image of an invalid courtier tottering about London streets in the time of the plague.

The portion of the narrative which, perhaps, most excited interest, as well as some surprise, considering the latitudes in question, was the long calms spoken of, and more particularly the ship's so long drifting about. Without communicating the opinion, of course, the American could not but impute at least part of the detentions both to clumsy seamanship and faulty navigation. Eying Don Benito's small, yellow hands, he easily inferred that the young captain had not got into command at the hawsehole, but the cabin-window; and if so, why wonder at incompetence, in youth, sickness, and gentility united?

But drowning criticism in compassion, after a fresh repetition of his sympathies, Captain Delano having heard out his story, not only engaged, as in the first place, to see Don Benito and his people supplied in their immediate bodily needs, but, also, now further promised to assist him in procuring a large permanent supply of water, as well as some sails and rigging; and, though it would involve no small embarrassment to himself, yet

---

10. *Ghetto:* A historical reference to the area of Rome to which Jews were restricted in the Renaissance and later.
11. *begging friar of St. Francis:* Whereas Dominicans were known as preaching friars, the Franciscans adopted a vow of poverty and made their way in the world through begging.

he would spare three of his best seamen for temporary deck officers; so that without delay the ship might proceed to Conception, there fully to refit for Lima, her destined port.

Such generosity was not without its effect, even upon the invalid. His face lighted up; eager and hectic, he met the honest glance of his visitor. With gratitude he seemed overcome.

"This excitement is bad for master," whispered the servant, taking his arm, and with soothing words gently drawing him aside.

When Don Benito returned, the American was pained to observe that his hopefulness, like the sudden kindling in his cheek, was but febrile and transient.

Ere long, with a joyless mien, looking up towards the poop, the host invited his guest to accompany him there, for the benefit of what little breath of wind might be stirring.

As during the telling of the story, Captain Delano had once or twice started at the occasional cymballing of the hatchet-polishers, wondering why such an interruption should be allowed, especially in that part of the ship, and in the ears of an invalid; and moreover, as the hatchets had anything but an attractive look, and the handlers of them still less so, it was, therefore, to tell the truth, not without some lurking reluctance, or even shrinking, it may be, that Captain Delano, with apparent complaisance, acquiesced in his host's invitation. The more so, since with an untimely caprice of punctilio, rendered distressing by his cadaverous aspect, Don Benito, with Castilian bows, solemnly insisted upon his guest's preceding him up the ladder leading to the elevation; where one on each side of the last step, sat for armorial supporters and sentries two of the ominous file. Gingerly enough stepped good Captain Delano between them, and in the instant of leaving them behind, like one running the gauntlet, he felt an apprehensive twitch in the calves of his legs.

But when, facing about, he saw the whole file, like so many organ-grinders, still stupidly intent on their work, unmindful of everything beside, he could not but smile at his late fidgeting panic.

Presently, while standing with his host, looking forward upon the decks below, he was struck by one of those instances of insubordination previously alluded to. Three black boys, with two Spanish boys, were sitting together on the hatches, scraping a rude wooden platter, in which some scanty mess had recently been cooked. Suddenly, one of the black boys, enraged at a word dropped by one of his white companions, seized a knife, and though called to forbear by one of the oakum-pickers, struck the lad over the head, inflicting a gash from which blood flowed.

In amazement, Captain Delano inquired what this meant. To which the pale Don Benito dully muttered, that it was merely the sport of the lad.

"Pretty serious sport, truly," rejoined Captain Delano. "Had such a thing happened on board the Bachelor's Delight, instant punishment would have followed."

At these words the Spaniard turned upon the American one of his sudden, staring, half-lunatic looks; then relapsing into his torpor, answered, "Doubtless, doubtless, Señor."

Is it, thought Captain Delano, that this hapless man is one of those paper captains I've known, who by policy wink at what by power they cannot put down? I know no sadder sight than a commander who has little of command but the name.

"I should think, Don Benito," he now said, glancing towards the oakum-picker who had sought to interfere with the boys, "that you would find it advantageous to keep all your blacks employed, especially the younger ones, no matter at what useless task, and no matter what happens to the ship. Why, even with my little band, I find such a course indispensable. I once kept a crew on my quarter-deck thrumming mats for my cabin, when, for three days, I had given up my ship — mats, men, and all — for a speedy loss, owing to the violence of a gale, in which we could do nothing but helplessly drive before it."

"Doubtless, doubtless," muttered Don Benito.

"But," continued Captain Delano, again glancing upon the oakum-pickers and then at the hatchet-polishers, near by, "I see you keep some at least of your host employed."

"Yes," was again the vacant response.

"Those old men there, shaking their pows[12] from their pulpits," continued Captain Delano, pointing to the oakum-pickers, "seem to act the part of old dominies to the rest, little heeded as their admonitions are at times. Is this voluntary on their part, Don Benito, or have you appointed them shepherds to your flock of black sheep?"

"What posts they fill, I appointed them," rejoined the Spaniard, in an acrid tone, as if resenting some supposed satiric reflection.

"And these others, these Ashantee conjurors here," continued Captain Delano, rather uneasily eying the brandished steel of the hatchet-polishers, where in spots it had been brought to a shine, "this seems a curious business they are at, Don Benito?"

---

12. *pows*: A Scottish dialect version of "polls" or "heads." Melville puns here on "dominies" (recurring to the references to Dominican orders and Santo Domingo) and "black sheep" (referring both to wicked sinners and African slaves).

"In the gales we met," answered the Spaniard, "what of our general cargo was not thrown overboard was much damaged by the brine. Since coming into calm weather, I have had several cases of knives and hatchets daily brought up for overhauling and cleaning."

"A prudent idea, Don Benito. You are part owner of ship and cargo, I presume; but not of the slaves, perhaps?"

"I am owner of all you see," impatiently returned Don Benito, "except the main company of blacks, who belonged to my late friend, Alexandro Aranda."

As he mentioned this name, his air was heart-broken; his knees shook: his servant supported him.

Thinking he divined the cause of such unusual emotion, to confirm his surmise, Captain Delano, after a pause, said, "And may I ask, Don Benito, whether — since awhile ago you spoke of some cabin passengers — the friend, whose loss so afflicts you at the outset of the voyage accompanied his blacks?"

"Yes."

"But died of the fever?"

"Died of the fever. — Oh, could I but —"

Again quivering, the Spaniard paused.

"Pardon me," said Captain Delano lowly, "but I think that, by a sympathetic experience, I conjecture, Don Benito, what it is that gives the keener edge to your grief. It was once my hard fortune to lose at sea a dear friend, my own brother, then supercargo. Assured of the welfare of his spirit, its departure I could have borne like a man; but that honest eye, that honest hand — both of which had so often met mine — and that warm heart; all, all — like scraps to the dogs — to throw all to the sharks! It was then I vowed never to have for fellow-voyager a man I loved, unless, unbeknown to him, I had provided every requisite, in case of a fatality, for embalming his mortal part for interment on shore. Were your friend's remains now on board this ship, Don Benito, not thus strangely would the mention of his name affect you."

"On board this ship?" echoed the Spaniard. Then, with horrified gestures, as directed against some specter, he unconsciously fell into the ready arms of his attendant, who, with a silent appeal toward Captain Delano, seemed beseeching him not again to broach a theme so unspeakably distressing to his master.

This poor fellow now, thought the pained American, is the victim of that sad superstition which associates goblins with the deserted body of man, as ghosts with an abandoned house. How unlike are we made! What to me, in like case, would have been a solemn satisfaction, the bare suggestion, even, terrifies the Spaniard into this trance. Poor Alexandro Aranda! what would you say could you here see your friend – who, on former voyages, when you for months were left behind, has, I dare say, often longed, and longed, for one peep at you – now transported with terror at the least thought of having you anyway nigh him.

At this moment, with a dreary grave-yard toll, betokening a flaw, the ship's forecastle bell, smote by one of the grizzled oakum-pickers, proclaimed ten o'clock through the leaden calm; when Captain Delano's attention was caught by the moving figure of a gigantic black, emerging from the general crowd below, and slowly advancing towards the elevated poop. An iron collar was about his neck, from which depended a chain, thrice wound round his body; the terminating links padlocked together at a broad band of iron, his girdle.

"How like a mute Atufal moves," murmured the servant.

The black mounted the steps of the poop, and, like a brave prisoner, brought up to receive sentence, stood in unquailing muteness before Don Benito, now recovered from his attack.

At the first glimpse of his approach, Don Benito had started, a resentful shadow swept over his face; and, as with the sudden memory of bootless rage, his white lips glued together.

This is some mulish mutineer, thought Captain Delano, surveying, not without a mixture of admiration, the colossal form of the negro.

"See, he waits your question, master," said the servant.

Thus reminded, Don Benito, nervously averting his glance, as if shunning, by anticipation, some rebellious response, in a disconcerted voice, thus spoke: –

"Atufal, will you ask my pardon now?"

The black was silent.

"Again, master," murmured the servant, with bitter upbraiding eying his countryman, "Again, master; he will bend to master yet."

"Answer," said Don Benito, still averting his glance, "say but the one world *pardon*, and your chains shall be off."

Upon this, the black, slowly raising both arms, let them lifelessly fall, his links clanking, his head bowed; as much as to say, "no, I am content."

"Go," said Don Benito, with inkept and unknown emotion.

Deliberately as he had come, the black obeyed.

"Excuse me, Don Benito," said Captain Delano, "but this scene surprises me; what means it, pray?"

"It means that that negro alone, of all the band, has given me peculiar cause of offense. I have put him in chains; I – "

Here he paused; his hand to his head, as if there were a swimming there, or a sudden bewilderment of memory had come over him; but meeting his servant's kindly glance seemed reassured, and proceeded: –

"I could not scourge such a form. But I told him he must ask my pardon. As yet he has not. At my command, every two hours he stands before me."

"And how long has this been?"

"Some sixty days."

"And obedient in all else? And respectful?"

"Yes."

"Upon my conscience, then," exclaimed Captain Delano, impulsively, "he has a royal spirit in him, this fellow."

"He may have some right to it," bitterly returned Don Benito, "he says he was king in his own land."

"Yes," said the servant, entering a word, "those slits in Atufal's ears once held wedges of gold; but poor Babo here, in his own land, was only a poor slave; a black man's slave was Babo, who now is the white's."

Somewhat annoyed by these conversational familiarities, Captain Delano turned curiously upon the attendant, then glanced inquiringly at his master; but, as if long wonted to these little informalities, neither master nor man seemed to understand him.

"What, pray, was Atufal's offense, Don Benito?" asked Captain Delano; "if it was not something very serious, take a fool's advice, and, in view of his general docility, as well as in some natural respect for his spirit, remit him his penalty."

"No, no, master never will do that," here murmured the servant to himself, "proud Atufal must first ask master's pardon. The slave there carries the padlock, but master here carries the key."

His attention thus directed, Captain Delano now noticed for the first time that, suspended by a slender silken cord, from Don Benito's neck hung a key. At once, from the servant's muttered syllables divining the key's purpose, he smiled and said: – "So, Don Benito – padlock and key – significant symbols, truly."

Biting his lip, Don Benito faltered.

Though the remark of Captain Delano, a man of such native simplicity as to be incapable of satire or irony, had been dropped in playful allusion to the Spaniard's singularly evidenced lordship over the black; yet the hypochondriac seemed in some way to have taken it as a malicious reflection upon his confessed inability thus far to break down, at least, on a verbal summons, the entrenched will of the slave. Deploring this supposed misconception, yet despairing of correcting it, Captain Delano shifted the subject; but finding his companion more than ever withdrawn, as if still sourly digesting the lees of the presumed affront above-mentioned, by-and-by Captain Delano likewise became less talkative, oppressed, against his own will, by what seemed the secret vindictiveness of the morbidly sensitive Spaniard. But the good sailor himself, of a quite contrary disposition, refrained, on his part, alike from the appearance as from the feeling of resentment, and if silent, was only so from contagion.

Presently the Spaniard, assisted by his servant, somewhat discourteously crossed over from his guest; a procedure which, sensibly enough, might have been allowed to pass for idle caprice of ill-humor, had not master and man, lingering round the corner of the elevated skylight, began [begun] whispering together in low voices. This was unpleasing. And more: the moody air of the Spaniard, which at times had not been without a sort of valetudinarian[13] stateliness, now seemed anything but dignified; while the menial familiarity of the servant lost its original charm of simple-hearted attachment.

In his embarrassment, the visitor turned his face to the other side of the ship. By so doing, his glance accidentally fell on a young Spanish sailor, a coil of rope in his hand, just stepped from the deck to the first round of the mizzen-rigging. Perhaps the man would not have been particularly noticed, were it not that, during his ascent to one of the yards, he, with a sort of covert intentness, kept his eye fixed on Captain Delano, from whom, presently, it passed, as if by a natural sequence, to the two whisperers.

His own attention thus redirected to that quarter, Captain Delano gave a slight start. From something in Don Benito's manner just then, it seemed as if the visitor had, at least partly, been the subject of the withdrawn consultation going on – a conjecture as little agreeable to the guest as it was little flattering to the host.

The singular alternations of courtesy and ill-breeding in the Spanish captain were unaccountable, except on one of two suppositions – innocent lunacy, or wicked imposture.

But the first idea, though it might naturally have occurred to an indifferent observer, and, in some respect, had not hitherto been wholly a stranger to Captain Delano's mind, yet, now that, in an incipient way, he began to regard the stranger's conduct something in the light of an intentional affront, of course the idea of lunacy was virtually vacated. But if not a lunatic, what then? Under the circumstances, would a gentleman, nay, any honest

---

13. *valetudinarian*: Having to do with or denoting ill health.

boor, act the part now acted by his host? The man was an impostor. Some low-born adventurer, masquerading as an oceanic grandee; yet so ignorant of the first requisites of mere gentlemanhood as to be betrayed into the present remarkable indecorum. That strange ceremoniousness, too, at other times evinced, seemed not uncharacteristic of one playing a part above his real level. Benito Cereno – Don Benito Cereno – a sounding name. One, too, at that period, not unknown, in the surname, to supercargoes and sea captains trading along the Spanish Main, as belonging to one of the most enterprising and extensive mercantile families in all those provinces; several members of it having titles; a sort of Castilian Rothschild, with a noble brother, or cousin, in every great trading town of South America. The alleged Don Benito was in early manhood, about twenty-nine or thirty. To assume a sort of roving cadetship in the maritime affairs of such a house, what more likely scheme for a young knave of talent and spirit? But the Spaniard was a pale invalid. Never mind. For even to the degree of simulating mortal disease, the craft of some tricksters had been known to attain. To think that, under the aspect of infantile weakness, the most savage energies might be couched – those velvets of the Spaniard but the silky paw to his fangs.

From no train of thought did these fancies come; not from within, but from without; suddenly, too, and in one throng, like hoar frost; yet as soon to vanish as the mild sun of Captain Delano's good-nature regained its meridian.

Glancing over once more towards his host – whose side-face, revealed above the skylight, was now turned towards him – he was struck by the profile, whose clearness of cut was refined by the thinness incident to ill-health, as well as ennobled about the chin by the beard. Away with suspicion. He was a true off-shoot of a true hidalgo Cereno.

Relieved by these and other better thoughts, the visitor, lightly humming a tune, now began indifferently pacing the poop, so as not to betray to Don Benito that he had at all mistrusted incivility, much less duplicity; for such mistrust would yet be proved illusory, and by the event; though, for the present, the circumstance which had provoked that distrust remained unexplained. But when that little mystery should have been cleared up, Captain Delano thought he might extremely regret it, did he allow Don Benito to become aware that he had indulged in ungenerous surmises. In short, to the Spaniard's black-letter text,[14] it was best, for awhile, to leave open margin.

---

14. *black-letter text*: An early typeface, introduced by printers in 1600, that resembled handwritten medieval texts.

Presently, his pale face twitching and overcast, the Spaniard, still supported by his attendant, moved over towards his guest, when, with even more than his usual embarrassment, and a strange sort of intriguing intonation in his husky whisper, the following conversation began: –

"Señor, may I ask how long you have lain at this isle?"

"Oh, but a day or two, Don Benito."

"And from what port are you last?"

"Canton."

"And there, Señor, you exchanged your seal-skins for teas and silks, I think you said?"

"Yes. Silks, mostly."

"And the balance you took in specie, perhaps?"

Captain Delano, fidgeting a little, answered –

"Yes; some silver; not a very great deal, though."

"Ah – well. May I ask how many men have you, Señor?"

Captain Delano slightly started, but answered –

"About five-and-twenty, all told."

"And at present, Señor, all on board, I suppose?"

"All on board, Don Benito," replied the Captain, now with satisfaction.

"And will be to-night, Señor?"

At this last question, following so many pertinacious ones, for the soul of him Captain Delano could not but look very earnestly at the questioner, who, instead of meeting the glance, with every token of craven discomposure dropped his eyes to the deck; presenting an unworthy contrast to his servant, who, just then, was kneeling at his feet, adjusting a loose shoe-buckle; his disengaged face meantime, with humble curiosity, turned openly up into his master's downcast one.

The Spaniard, still with a guilty shuffle, repeated his question: –

"And – and will be to-night, Señor?"

"Yes, for aught I know," returned Captain Delano, – "but nay," rallying himself into fearless truth, "some of them talked of going off on another fishing party about midnight."

"Your ships generally go – go more or less armed, I believe, Señor?"

"Oh, a six-pounder or two, in case of emergency," was the intrepidly indifferent reply, "with a small stock of muskets, sealing-spears, and cutlasses, you know."

As he thus responded, Captain Delano again glanced at Don Benito, but the latter's eyes were averted; while abruptly and awkwardly shifting the subject, he made some peevish allusion to the calm, and then, without apology, once more, with his attendant, withdrew to the opposite bulwarks, where the whispering was resumed.

At this moment, and ere Captain Delano could cast a cool thought upon what had just passed, the young Spanish sailor before mentioned was seen descending from the rigging. In act of stooping over to spring inboard to the deck, his voluminous, unconfined frock, or shirt, of coarse woollen, much spotted with tar, opened out far down the chest, revealing a soiled under garment of what seemed the finest linen, edged, about the neck, with a narrow blue ribbon, sadly faded and worn. At this moment the young sailor's eye was again fixed on the whisperers, and Captain Delano thought he observed a lurking significance in it, as if silent signs of some Freemason[15] sort had that instant been interchanged.

This once more impelled his own glance in the direction of Don Benito, and, as before, he could not but infer that himself formed the subject of the conference. He paused. The sound of the hatchet-polishing fell on his ears. He cast another swift side-look at the two. They had the air of conspirators. In connection with the late questionings and the incident of the young sailor, these things now begat such return of involuntary suspicion, that the singular guilelessness of the American could not endure it. Plucking up a gay and humorous expression, he crossed over to the two rapidly, saying: – "Ha, Don Benito, your black here seems high in your trust; a sort of privy-counselor, in fact."

Upon this, the servant looked up with a good-natured grin, but the master started as from a venomous bite. It was a moment or two before the Spaniard sufficiently recovered himself to reply; which he did, at last, with cold constraint: – "Yes, Señor, I have trust in Babo."

Here Babo, changing his previous grin of mere animal humor into an intelligent smile, not ungratefully eyed his master.

Finding that the Spaniard now stood silent and reserved, as if involuntarily, or purposely giving hint that his guest's proximity was inconvenient just then, Captain Delano, unwilling to appear uncivil even to incivility itself, made some trivial remark and moved off; again and again turning over in his mind the mysterious demeanor of Don Benito Cereno.

He had descended from the poop, and, wrapped in thought, was passing near a dark hatchway, leading down into the steerage, when, perceiving

---

15. *Freemason:* A member of a secret fraternal organization founded in the seventeenth century to protect the history and symbols of medieval craft guilds. By the nineteenth century in America, this organization was associated by some Americans with antidemocratic and heretical movements in Europe.

motion there, he looked to see what moved. The same instant there was a
sparkle in the shadowy hatchway, and he saw one of the Spanish sailors
prowling there hurriedly placing his hand in the bosom of his frock, as if
hiding something. Before the man could have been certain who it was that
was passing, he slunk below out of sight. But enough was seen of him to
make it sure that he was the same young sailor before noticed in the rigging.

What was that which so sparkled? thought Captain Delano. It was no
lamp – no match – no live coal. Could it have been a jewel? But how come
sailors with jewels? – or with silk-trimmed under-shirts either? Has he been
robbing the trunks of the dead cabin passengers? But if so, he would hardly
wear one of the stolen articles on board ship here. Ah, ah – if now that was,
indeed, a secret sign I saw passing between this suspicious fellow and his
captain awhile since; if I could only be certain that in my uneasiness my
senses did not deceive me, then –

Here, passing from one suspicious thing to another, his mind revolved
the point of the strange questions put to him concerning his ship.

By a curious coincidence, as each point was recalled, the black wiz-
ards of Ashantee would strike up with their hatchets, as in ominous comment
on the white stranger's thoughts. Pressed by such enigmas and portents, it
would have been almost against nature, had not, even into the least dis-
trustful heart, some ugly misgivings obtruded.

Observing the ship now helplessly fallen into a current, with enchanted
sails, drifting with increased rapidity seaward; and noting that, from a lately
intercepted projection of the land, the sealer was hidden, the stout mariner
began to quake at thoughts which he barely durst confess to himself.
Above all, he began to feel a ghostly dread of Don Benito. And yet when he
roused himself, dilated his chest, felt himself strong on his legs, and coolly
considered it – what did all these phantoms amount to?

Had the Spaniard any sinister scheme, it must have reference not so
much to him (Captain Delano) as to his ship (the Bachelor's Delight). Hence
the present drifting away of the one ship from the other, instead of favor-
ing any such possible scheme, was, for the time at least, opposed to it.
Clearly any suspicion, combining such contradictions, must need be delu-
sive. Beside, was it not absurd to think of a vessel in distress – a vessel by
sickness almost dismanned of her crew – a vessel whose inmates were
parched for water – was it not a thousand times absurd that such a craft
should, at present, be of a piratical character; or her commander, either for
himself or those under him, cherish any desire but for speedy relief and
refreshment? But then, might not general distress, and thirst in particular,
be affected? And might not that same undiminished Spanish crew, alleged

to have perished off to a remnant, be at that very moment lurking in the hold? On heart-broken pretense of entreating a cup of cold water, fiends in human form had got into lonely dwellings, nor retired until a dark deed had been done. And among the Malay pirates, it was no unusual thing to lure ships after them into their treacherous harbors, or entice boarders from a declared enemy at sea, by the spectacle of thinly manned or vacant decks, beneath which prowled a hundred spears with yellow arms ready to upthrust them through the mats. Not that Captain Delano had entirely credited such things. He had heard of them – and now, as stories, they recurred. The present destination of the ship was the anchorage. There she would be near his own vessel. Upon gaining that vicinity, might not the San Dominick, like a slumbering volcano,[16] suddenly let loose energies now hid?

He recalled the Spaniard's manner while telling his story. There was a gloomy hesitancy and subterfuge about it. It was just the manner of one making up his tale for evil purposes, as he goes. But if that story was not true, what was the truth? That the ship had unlawfully come into the Spaniard's possession? But in many of its details, especially in reference to the more calamitous parts, such as the fatalities among the seamen, the consequent prolonged beating about, the past sufferings from obstinate calms, and still continued suffering from thirst; in all these points, as well as others, Don Benito's story had been corroborated not only by the wailing ejaculations of the indiscriminate multitude, white and black, but likewise – what seemed impossible to be counterfeit – by the very expression and play of every human feature, which Captain Delano saw. If Don Benito's story was throughout an invention, then every soul on board, down to the youngest negress, was his carefully drilled recruit in the plot: an incredible inference. And yet, if there was ground for mistrusting his veracity, that inference was a legitimate one.

But those questions of the Spaniard. There, indeed, one might pause. Did they not seem put with much the same object with which the burglar or assassin, by day-time, reconnoitres the walls of a house? But, with ill purposes, to solicit such information openly of the chief person endangered, and so, in effect, setting him on his guard; how unlikely a procedure was that? Absurd, then, to suppose that those questions had been prompted by evil designs. Thus, the same conduct, which, in this instance, had raised the alarm, served to dispel it. In short, scarce any suspicion or uneasiness, however apparently reasonable at the time, which was not now, with equal apparent reason, dismissed.

---

16. *slumbering volcano*: Phrase used in the title of a speech by Frederick Douglass in April 1849.

At last he began to laugh at his former forebodings; and laugh at the strange ship for, in its aspect someway siding with them, as it were; and laugh, too, at the odd-looking blacks, particularly those old scissors-grinders, the Ashantees; and those bed-ridden old knitting-women, the oakum-pickers; and almost at the dark Spaniard himself, the central hobgoblin of all.

For the rest, whatever in a serious way seemed enigmatical, was now good-naturedly explained away by the thought that, for the most part, the poor invalid scarcely knew what he was about; either sulking in black vapors, or putting idle questions without sense or object. Evidently, for the present, the man was not fit to be entrusted with the ship. On some benevolent plea withdrawing the command from him, Captain Delano would yet have to send her to Conception, in charge of his second mate, a worthy person and good navigator – a plan not more convenient for the San Dominick than for Don Benito; for, relieved from all anxiety, keeping wholly to his cabin, the sick man, under the good nursing of his servant, would probably, by the end of the passage, be in a measure restored to health, and with that he should also be restored to authority.

Such were the American's thoughts. They were tranquilizing. There was a difference between the idea of Don Benito's darkly pre-ordaining Captain Delano's fate, and Captain Delano's lightly arranging Don Benito's. Nevertheless, it was not without something of relief that the good seaman presently perceived his whale-boat in the distance. Its absence had been prolonged by unexpected detention at the sealer's side, as well as its returning trip lengthened by the continual recession of the goal.

The advancing speck was observed by the blacks. Their shouts attracted the attention of Don Benito, who, with a return of courtesy, approaching Captain Delano, expressed satisfaction at the coming of some supplies, slight and temporary as they must necessarily prove.

Captain Delano responded; but while doing so, his attention was drawn to something passing on the deck below: among the crowd climbing the landward bulwarks, anxiously watching the coming boat, two blacks, to all appearances accidentally incommoded by one of the sailors, flew out against him with horrible curses, which the sailor someway resenting, the two blacks dashed him to the deck and jumped upon him, despite the earnest cries of the oakum-pickers.

"Don Benito," said Captain Delano quickly, "do you see what is going on there? Look!"

But, seized by his cough, the Spaniard staggered, with both hands to his face, on the point of falling. Captain Delano would have supported him, but the servant was more alert, who, with one hand sustaining his master, with the other applied the cordial. Don Benito restored, the black withdrew his support, slipping aside a little, but dutifully remaining within call of a whisper. Such discretion was here evinced as quite wiped away, in the visitor's eyes, any blemish of impropriety which might have attached to the attendant, from the indecorous conferences before mentioned; showing, too, that if the servant were to blame, it might be more the master's fault than his own, since when left to himself he could conduct thus well.

His glance thus called away from the spectacle of disorder to the more pleasing one before him, Captain Delano could not avoid again congratulating his host upon possessing such a servant, who, though perhaps a little too forward now and then, must upon the whole be invaluable to one in the invalid's situation.

"Tell me, Don Benito," he added, with a smile – "I should like to have your man here myself – what will you take for him? Would fifty doubloons be any object?"

"Master wouldn't part with Babo for a thousand doubloons," murmured the black, overhearing the offer, and taking it in earnest, and, with the strange vanity of a faithful slave appreciated by his master, scorning to hear so paltry a valuation put upon him by a stranger. But Don Benito, apparently hardly yet completely restored, and again interrupted by his cough, made but some broken reply.

Soon his physical distress became so great, affecting his mind, too, apparently, that, as if to screen the sad spectacle, the servant gently conducted his master below.

Left to himself, the American, to while away the time till his boat should arrive, would have pleasantly accosted some one of the few Spanish seamen he saw; but recalling something that Don Benito had said touching their ill conduct, he refrained, as a ship-master indisposed to countenance cowardice or unfaithfulness in seamen.

While, with these thoughts, standing with eye directed forward towards that handful of sailors, suddenly he thought that one or two of them returned the glance and with a sort of meaning. He rubbed his eyes, and looked again; but again seemed to see the same thing. Under a new form, but more obscure than any previous one, the old suspicions recurred, but, in the absence of Don Benito, with less of panic than before. Despite the bad account given of the sailors, Captain Delano resolved forthwith to accost one of them. Descending the poop, he made his way through the blacks, his movement drawing a queer cry from the oakum-pickers, prompted by whom, the negroes, twitching each other aside, divided before him; but, as if curious to see what was the object of this deliberate visit to their Ghetto, closing in behind, in tolerable order, followed the white stranger up. His progress thus proclaimed as by mounted kings-at-arms, and escorted as by a Caffre[17] guard of honor, Captain Delano, assuming a good humored, off-handed air, continued to advance; now and then saying a blithe word to the negroes, and his eye curiously surveying the white faces, here and there sparsely mixed in with the blacks, like stray white pawns venturously involved in the ranks of the chess-men opposed.

While thinking which of them to select for his purpose, he chanced to observe a sailor seated on the deck engaged in tarring the strap of a large block, with a circle of blacks squatted round him inquisitively eying the process.

The mean employment of the man was in contrast with something superior in his figure. His hand, black with continually thrusting it into the tar-pot held for him by a negro, seemed not naturally allied to his face, a face which would have been a very fine one but for its haggardness. Whether this haggardness had aught to do with criminality, could not be determined; since, as intense heat and cold, though unlike, produce like sensations, so innocence and guilt, when, through casual association with mental pain, stamping any visible impress, use one seal – a hacked one.

Not again that this reflection occurred to Captain Delano at the time, charitable man as he was. Rather another idea. Because observing so singular a haggardness combined with a dark eye, averted as in trouble and shame, and then again recalling Don Benito's confessed ill opinion of his crew, insensibly he was operated upon by certain general notions, which, while disconnecting pain and abashment from virtue, invariably link them with vice.

If, indeed, there be any wickedness on board this ship, thought Captain Delano, be sure that man there has fouled his hand in it, even as now he fouls it in the pitch. I don't like to accost him. I will speak to this other, this old Jack here on the windlass.

He advanced to an old Barcelona tar, in ragged red breeches and dirty night-cap, cheeks trenched and bronzed, whiskers dense as thorn hedges. Seated between two sleepy-looking Africans, this mariner, like his younger shipmate, was employed upon some rigging – splicing a cable – the sleepy-looking blacks performing the inferior function of holding the outer parts of the ropes for him.

---

17. *Caffre*: From Arab *kaffir*, meaning a non-Muslim or infidel. Here more likely used to refer to a member of a group of Southern African Bantu-speaking peoples or, more generally, a black African.

Upon Captain Delano's approach, the man at once hung his head below its previous level; the one necessary for business. It appeared as if he desired to be thought absorbed, with more than common fidelity, in his task. Being addressed, he glanced up, but with what seemed a furtive, diffident air, which sat strangely enough on his weather-beaten visage, much as if a grizzly bear, instead of growling and biting, should simper and cast sheep's eyes. He was asked several questions concerning the voyage, questions purposely referring to several particulars in Don Benito's narrative, not previously corroborated by those impulsive cries greeting the visitor on first coming on board. The questions were briefly answered, confirming all that remained to be confirmed of the story. The negroes about the windlass joined in with the old sailor, but, as they became talkative, he by degrees became mute, and at length quite glum, seemed morosely unwilling to answer more questions, and yet, all the while, this ursine air was somehow mixed with his sheepish one.

Despairing of getting into unembarrassed talk with such a centaur, Captain Delano, after glancing round for a more promising countenance, but seeing none, spoke pleasantly to the blacks to make way for him; and so, amid various grins and grimaces, returned to the poop, feeling a little strange at first, he could hardly tell why, but upon the whole with regained confidence in Benito Cereno.

How plainly, thought he, did that old whiskerando yonder betray a consciousness of ill-desert. No doubt, when he saw me coming, he dreaded lest I, apprised by his Captain of the crew's general misbehavior, came with sharp words for him, and so down with his head. And yet – and yet, now that I think of it, that very old fellow, if I err not, was one of those who seemed so earnestly eying me here awhile since. Ah, these currents spin one's head round almost as much as they do the ship. Ha, there now's a pleasant sort of sunny sight; quite sociable, too.

His attention had been drawn to a slumbering negress, partly disclosed through the lace-work of some rigging, lying, with youthful limbs carelessly disposed, under the lee of the bulwarks, like a doe in the shade of a woodland rock. Sprawling at her lapped breasts was her wide-awake fawn, stark naked, its black little body half lifted from the deck, crosswise with its dam's; its hands, like two paws, clambering upon her; its mouth and nose ineffectually rooting to get at the mark; and meantime giving a vexatious half-grunt, blending with the composed snore of the negress.

The uncommon vigor of the child at length roused the mother. She started up, at distance facing Captain Delano. But as if not at all concerned at the attitude in which she had been caught, delightedly she caught the child up, with maternal transports, covering it with kisses.

There's naked nature, now; pure tenderness and love, thought Captain Delano, well pleased.

This incident prompted him to remark the other negresses more particularly than before. He was gratified with their manners; like most uncivilized women, they seemed at once tender of heart and tough of constitution; equally ready to die for their infants or fight for them. Unsophisticated as leopardesses; loving as doves. Ah! thought Captain Delano, these perhaps are some of the very women whom Mungo Park[18] saw in Africa, and gave such a noble account of. *very delwn zny (pahron zny*

These natural sights somehow insensibly deepened his confidence and ease. At last he looked to see how his boat was getting on; but it was still pretty remote. He turned to see if Don Benito had returned; but he had not.

To change the scene, as well as to please himself with a leisurely observation of the coming boat, stepping over into the mizzen-chains he clambered his way into the starboard quarter-gallery; one of those abandoned Venetian-looking water-balconies previously mentioned; retreats cut off from the deck. As his foot pressed the half-damp, half-dry sea-mosses matting the place, and a chance phantom cats-paw – an islet of breeze, unheralded, unfollowed – as this ghostly cats-paw came fanning his cheek, as his glance fell upon the row of small, round dead-lights, all closed like coppered eyes of the coffined, and the state-cabin door, once connecting with the gallery, even as the dead-lights had once looked out upon it, but now calked fast like a sarcophagus lid, to a purple-black, tarred-over panel, threshold, and post; and he bethought him of the time, when that state-cabin and this state-balcony had heard the voices of the Spanish king's officers, and the forms of the Lima viceroy's daughters had perhaps leaned where he stood – as these and other images flitted through his mind, as the cats-paw through the calm, gradually he felt rising a dreamy inquietude, like that of one who alone on the prairie feels unrest from the repose of the noon.

He leaned against the carved balustrade, again looking off toward his boat; but found his eye falling upon the ribbon grass, trailing along the ship's water-line, straight as a border of green box; and parterres of seaweed, broad ovals and crescents, floating nigh and far, with what seemed long formal alleys between, crossing the terraces of swells, and sweeping

18. *Mungo Park:* Melville used this name in the first version of *Benito Cereno* published in *Putnam's*, referring to the Scottish explorer (1771-1806) and author of *Travels in the Interior Districts of Africa* (1799). In 1856, the editors of *The Piazza Tales* mistakenly substituted the name of John Ledyard (1751-1789). The original name was restored here.

round as if leading to the grottoes below. And overhanging all was the balustrade by his arm, which, partly stained with pitch and partly embossed with moss, seemed the charred ruin of some summer-house in a grand garden long running to waste.

Trying to break one charm, he was but becharmed anew. Though upon the wide sea, he seemed in some far inland country; prisoner in some deserted château, left to stare at empty grounds, and peer out at vague roads, where never wagon or wayfarer passed.

But these enchantments were a little disenchanted as his eye fell on the corroded main-chains. Of an ancient style, massy and rusty in link, shackle and bolt, they seemed even more fit for the ship's present business than the one for which probably she had been built.

Presently he thought something moved nigh the chains. He rubbed his eyes, and looked hard. Groves of rigging were about the chains; and there, peering from behind a great stay, like an Indian from behind a hemlock, a Spanish sailor, a marlingspike in his hand, was seen, who made what seemed an imperfect gesture towards the balcony, but immediately, as if alarmed by some advancing step along the deck within, vanished into the recesses of the hempen forest, like a poacher.

What meant this? Something the man had sought to communicate, unbeknown to any one, even to his captain. Did the secret involve aught unfavorable to his captain? Were those previous misgivings of Captain Delano's about to be verified? Or, in his haunted mood at the moment, had some random, unintentional motion of the man, while busy with the stay, as if repairing it, been mistaken for a significant beckoning?

Not unbewildered, again he gazed off for his boat. But it was temporarily hidden by a rocky spur of the isle. As with some eagerness he bent forward, watching for the first shooting view of its beak, the balustrade gave way before him like charcoal. Had he not clutched an outreaching rope he would have fallen into the sea. The crash, though feeble, and the fall, though hollow, of the rotten fragments, must have been overheard. He glanced up. With sober curiosity peering down upon him was one of the old oakum-pickers, slipped from his perch to an outside boom; while below the old negro, and, invisible to him, reconnoitering from a porthole like a fox from the mouth of its den, crouched the Spanish sailor again. From something suddenly suggested by the man's air, the mad idea now darted into Captain Delano's mind, that Don Benito's plea of indisposition, in withdrawing below, was but a pretense: that he was engaged there maturing some plot, of which the sailor, by some means gaining an inkling, had a mind to warn the stranger against; incited, it may be, by gratitude for a kind word on first boarding the ship. Was it from foreseeing some possible interferer this, that Don Benito had, beforehand, given such a bad character of his sailors, while praising the negroes; though, indeed, the former seemed as docile as the latter the contrary? The whites, too, by nature, were the shrewder race. A man with some evil design, would he not be likely to speak well of that stupidity which was blind to his depravity, and malign that intelligence from which it might not be hidden? Not unlikely, perhaps. But if the whites had dark secrets concerning Don Benito, could then Don Benito be any way in complicity with the blacks? But they were too stupid. Besides, who ever heard of a white so far a renegade as to apostatize from his very species almost, by leaguing in against it with negroes? These difficulties recalled former ones. Lost in their mazes, Captain Delano, who had now regained the deck, was uneasily advancing along it, when he observed a new face; an aged sailor seated cross-legged near the main hatchway. His skin was shrunk up with wrinkles like a pelican's empty pouch; his hair frosted; his countenance grave and composed. His hands were full of ropes, which he was working into a large knot. Some blacks were about him obligingly dipping the strands for him, here and there, as the exigencies of the operation demanded.

Captain Delano crossed over to him, and stood in silence surveying the knot; his mind, by a not uncongenial transition, passing from its own entanglements to those of the hemp. For intricacy such a knot he had never seen in an American ship, or indeed any other. The old man looked like an Egyptian priest, making gordian knots[19] for the temple of Ammon. The knot seemed a combination of double-bowline-knot, treble-crown-knot, back-handed-well-knot, knot-in-and-out-knot, and jamming-knot.

At last, puzzled to comprehend the meaning of such a knot, Captain Delano addressed the knotter: –

"What are you knotting there, my man?"

"The knot," was the brief reply, without looking up.

"So it seems; but what is it for?"

"For some one else to undo," muttered back the old man, plying his fingers harder than ever, the knot being now nearly completed.

While Captain Delano stood watching him, suddenly the old man threw the knot towards him, saying in broken English, – the first heard in the ship, – something to this effect – "Undo it, cut it, quick." It was said lowly, but with such condensation of rapidity, that the long, slow words in

---

19. *gordian knots*: Alexander the Great cut the Gordian knot in 333 B.C.E., then in 332 visited the temple of Ammon in Egypt.

Spanish, which had preceded and followed, almost operated as covers to the brief English between.

For a moment, knot in hand, and knot in head, Captain Delano stood mute; while, without further heeding him, the old man was now intent upon other ropes. Presently there was a slight stir behind Captain Delano. Turning, he saw the chained negro, Atufal, standing quietly there. The next moment the old sailor rose, muttering, and, followed by his subordinate negroes, removed to the forward part of the ship, where in the crowd he disappeared.

An elderly negro, in a clout like an infant's, and with a pepper and salt head, and a kind of attorney air, now approached Captain Delano. In tolerable Spanish, and with a good-natured, knowing wink, he informed him that the old knotter was simple-witted, but harmless; often playing his old tricks. The negro concluded by begging the knot, for of course the stranger would not care to be troubled with it. Unconsciously, it was handed to him. With a sort of congé, the negro received it, and turning his back, ferreted into it like a detective Custom House officer after smuggled laces. Soon, with some African word, equivalent to pshaw, he tossed the knot overboard.

All this is very queer now, thought Captain Delano, with a qualmish sort of emotion; but as one feeling incipient sea-sickness, he strove, by ignoring the symptoms, to get rid of the malady. Once more he looked off for his boat. To his delight, it was now again in view, leaving the rocky spur astern.

The sensation here experienced, after at first relieving his uneasiness, with unforeseen efficacy, soon began to remove it. The less distant sight of that well-known boat – showing it, not as before, half blended with the haze, but with outline defined, so that its individuality, like a man's, was manifest; that boat, Rover by name, which, though now in strange seas, had often pressed the beach of Captain Delano's home, and, brought to its threshold for repairs, had familiarly lain there, as a Newfoundland dog; the sight of that household boat evoked a thousand trustful associations, which, contrasted with previous suspicions, filled him not only with lightsome confidence, but somehow with half humorous self-reproaches at his former lack of it.

"What, I, Amasa Delano – Jack of the Beach, as they called me when a lad – I, Amasa; the same that, duck-satchel in hand, used to paddle along the waterside to the school-house made from the old hulk; – I, little Jack of the Beach, that used to go berrying with cousin Nat and the rest; I to be murdered here at the ends of the earth, on board a haunted pirate-ship by a horrible Spaniard? – Too nonsensical to think of! Who would murder Amasa Delano? His conscience is clean. There is some one above. Fie, fie, Jack of the Beach! you are a child indeed; a child of the second childhood, old boy; you are beginning to dote and drule, I'm afraid."

Light of heart and foot, he stepped aft, and there was met by Don Benito's servant, who, with a pleasing expression, responsive to his own present feelings, informed him that his master had recovered from the effects of his coughing fit, and had just ordered him to go present his compliments to his good guest, Don Amasa, and say that he (Don Benito) would soon have the happiness to rejoin him.

There now, do you mark that? again thought Captain Delano, walking the poop. What a donkey I was. This kind gentleman who here sends me his kind compliments, he, but ten minutes ago, dark-lantern in hand, was dodging round some old grind-stone in the hold, sharpening a hatchet for me, I thought. Well, well; these long calms have a morbid effect on the mind, I've often heard, though I never believed it before. Ha! glancing towards the boat; there's Rover; good dog; a white bone in her mouth. A pretty big bone though, seems to me. – What? Yes, she has fallen afoul of the bubbling tide-rip there. It sets her the other way, too, for the time. Patience.

It was now about noon, though, from the grayness of everything, it seemed to be getting towards dusk.

The calm was confirmed. In the far distance, away from the influence of land, the leaden ocean seemed laid out and leaded up, its course finished, soul gone, defunct. But the current from landward, where the ship was, increased; silently sweeping her further and further towards the tranced waters beyond.

Still, from his knowledge of those latitudes, cherishing hopes of a breeze, and a fair and fresh one, at any moment, Captain Delano, despite present prospects, buoyantly counted upon bringing the San Dominick safely to anchor ere night. The distance swept over was nothing; since, with a good wind, ten minutes' sailing would retrace more than sixty minutes' drifting. Meantime, one moment turning to mark "Rover" fighting the tide-rip, and the next to see Don Benito approaching, he continued walking the poop.

Gradually he felt a vexation arising from the delay of his boat; this soon merged into uneasiness; and at last, his eye falling continually, as from a stage-box into the pit, upon the strange crowd before and below him, and by and by recognising there the face – now composed to indifference – of the Spanish sailor who had seemed to beckon from the main chains, something of his old trepidations returned.

Ah, thought he – gravely enough – this is like the ague: because it went off, it follows not that it won't come back.

Though ashamed of the relapse, he could not altogether subdue it; and so, exerting his good nature to the utmost, insensibly he came to a compromise.

Yes, this is a strange craft; a strange history, too, and strange folks on board. But – nothing more.

By way of keeping his mind out of mischief till the boat should arrive, he tried to occupy it with turning over and over, in a purely speculative sort of way, some lesser peculiarities of the captain and crew. Among others, four curious points recurred.

First, the affair of the Spanish lad assailed with a knife by the slave boy; an act winked at by Don Benito. Second, the tyranny in Don Benito's treatment of Atufal, the black; as if a child should lead a bull of the Nile by the ring in his nose. Third, the trampling of the sailor by the two negroes; a piece of insolence passed over without so much as a reprimand. Fourth, the cringing submission to their master of all the ship's underlings, mostly blacks; as if by the least inadvertence they feared to draw down his despotic displeasure.

Coupling these points, they seemed somewhat contradictory. But what then, thought Captain Delano, glancing towards his now nearing boat, – what then? Why, Don Benito is a very capricious commander. But he is not the first of the sort I have seen; though it's true he rather exceeds any other. But as a nation – continued he in his reveries – these Spaniards are all an odd set; the very word Spaniard has a curious, conspirator, Guy-Fawkish[20] twang to it. And yet, I dare say, Spaniards in the main are as good folks as any in Duxbury, Massachusetts. Ah good! At last "Rover" has come.

As, with its welcome freight, the boat touched the side, the oakum-pickers, with venerable gestures, sought to restrain the blacks, who, at the sight of three gurried water-casks in its bottom, and a pile of wilted pumpkins in its bow, hung over the bulwarks in disorderly raptures.

Don Benito with his servant now appeared; his coming, perhaps, hastened by hearing the noise. Of him Captain Delano sought permission to serve out the water, so that all might share alike, and none injure themselves by unfair excess. But sensible, and, on Don Benito's account, kind as this offer was, it was received with what seemed impatience; as if aware that he lacked energy as a commander, Don Benito, with the true jealousy of weakness, resented as an affront any interference. So, at least, Captain Delano inferred.

---

20. *Guy-Fawkish:* Guy Fawkes (1570-1606), a Catholic, helped engineer the Gunpowder Plot (1605), a conspiracy to blow up Parliament and ignite a Catholic rebellion in England.

In another moment the casks were being hoisted in, when some of the eager negroes accidentally jostled Captain Delano, where he stood by the gangway; so that, unmindful of Don Benito, yielding to the impulse of the moment, with good-natured authority he bade the blacks stand back; to enforce his words making use of a half-mirthful, half-menacing gesture. Instantly the blacks paused, just where they were, each negro and negress suspended in his or her posture, exactly as the word had found them – for a few seconds continuing so – while, as between the responsive posts of a telegraph, an unknown syllable ran from man to man among the perched oakum-pickers. While the visitor's attention was fixed by this scene, suddenly the hatchet-polishers half rose, and a rapid cry came from Don Benito.

Thinking that at the signal of the Spaniard he was about to be massacred, Captain Delano would have sprung for his boat, but paused, as the oakum-pickers, dropping down into the crowd with earnest exclamations, forced every white and every negro back, at the same moment, with gestures friendly and familiar, almost jocose, bidding him, in substance, not be a fool. Simultaneously the hatchet-polishers resumed their seats, quietly as so many tailors, and at once, as if nothing had happened, the work of hoisting in the casks was resumed, whites and blacks singing at the tackle.

Captain Delano glanced towards Don Benito. As he saw his meager form in the act of recovering itself from reclining in the servant's arms, into which the agitated invalid had fallen, he could not but marvel at the panic by which himself had been surprised on the darting supposition that such a commander, who upon a legitimate occasion, so trivial, too, as it now appeared, could lose all self-command, was, with energetic iniquity, going to bring about his murder.

The casks being on deck, Captain Delano was handed a number of jars and cups by one of the steward's aids, who, in the name of his captain, entreated him to do as he had proposed: dole out the water. He complied, with republican impartiality as to this republican element, which always seeks one level, serving the oldest white no better than the youngest black; excepting, indeed, poor Don Benito, whose condition, if not rank, demanded an extra allowance. To him, in the first place, Captain Delano presented a fair pitcher of the fluid; but, thirsting as he was for it, the Spaniard quaffed not a drop until after several grave bows and salutes. A reciprocation of courtesies which the sight-loving Africans hailed with clapping of hands.

Two of the less wilted pumpkins being reserved for the cabin table, the residue were minced up on the spot for the general regalement. But the soft bread, sugar, and bottled cider, Captain Delano would have given the whites alone, and in chief Don Benito; but the latter objected; which disinterestedness, on his part, not a little pleased the American; and so mouthfuls all around were given alike to whites and blacks; excepting one bottle of cider, which Babo insisted upon setting aside for his master.

Here it may be observed that as, on the first visit of the boat, the American had not permitted his men to board the ship, neither did he now; being unwilling to add to the confusion of the decks.

Not uninfluenced by the peculiar good humor at present prevailing, and for the time oblivious of any but benevolent thoughts, Captain Delano, who from recent indications counted upon a breeze within an hour or two at furthest, dispatched the boat back to the sealer with orders for all the hands that could be spared immediately to set about rafting casks to the watering-place and filling them. Likewise he bade word be carried to his chief officer, that if against present expectation the ship was not brought to anchor by sunset, he need be under no concern, for as there was to be a full moon that night, he (Captain Delano) would remain on board ready to play the pilot, come the wind soon or late.

As the two Captains stood together, observing the departing boat – the servant as it happened having just spied a spot on his master's velvet sleeve, and silently engaged rubbing it out – the American expressed his regrets that the San Dominick had no boats; none, at least, but the unseaworthy old hulk of the long-boat, which, warped as a camel's skeleton in the desert, and almost as bleached, lay pot-wise inverted amidships, one side a little tipped, furnishing a subterraneous sort of den for family groups of the blacks, mostly women and small children; who, squatting on old mats below, or perched above in the dark dome, on the elevated seats, were descried, some distance within, like a social circle of bats, sheltering in some friendly cave; at intervals, ebon flights of naked boys and girls, three or four years old, darting in and out of the den's mouth.

"Had you three or four boats now, Don Benito," said Captain Delano, "I think that, by tugging at the oars, your negroes here might help along matters some. – Did you sail from port without boats, Don Benito?"

"They were stove in the gales, Señor."

"That was bad. Many men, too, you lost then. Boats and men. – Those must have been hard gales, Don Benito."

"Past all speech," cringed the Spaniard.

"Tell me, Don Benito," continued his companion with increased interest, "tell me, were these gales immediately off the pitch of Cape Horn?"

"Cape Horn? – who spoke of Cape Horn?"

"Yourself did, when giving me an account of your voyage," answered Captain Delano with almost equal astonishment at this eating of his own

words, even as he ever seemed eating his own heart, on the part of the
Spaniard. "You yourself, Don Benito, spoke of Cape Horn," he emphatically
repeated.

The Spaniard turned, in a sort of stooping posture, pausing an instant,
as one about to make a plunging exchange of elements, as from air to
water.

At this moment a messenger-boy, a white, hurried by, in the regular
performance of his function carrying the last expired half hour forward to
the forecastle, from the cabin time-piece, to have it struck at the ship's
large bell.

"Master," said the servant, discontinuing his work on the coat sleeve,
and addressing the rapt Spaniard with a sort of timid apprehensiveness,
as one charged with a duty, the discharge of which, it was foreseen, would
prove irksome to the very person who had imposed it, and for whose benefit it was intended, "master told me never mind where he was, or how engaged,
always to remind him, to a minute, when shaving-time comes. Miguel has
gone to strike the half-hour afternoon. It is now, master. Will master go
into the cuddy?"

"Ah — yes," answered the Spaniard, starting, somewhat as from dreams
into realities; then turning upon Captain Delano, he said that ere long he
would resume the conversation.

"Then if master means to talk more to Don Amasa," said the servant,
"why not let Don Amasa sit by master in the cuddy, and master can talk,
and Don Amasa can listen, while Babo here lathers and strops."

"Yes," said Captain Delano, not unpleased with this sociable plan, "yes,
Don Benito, unless you had rather not, I will go with you."

"Be it so, Señor."

As the three passed aft, the American could not but think it another
strange instance of his host's capriciousness, this being shaved with such
uncommon punctuality in the middle of the day. But he deemed it more
than likely that the servant's anxious fidelity had something to do with
the matter; inasmuch as the timely interruption served to rally his master
from the mood which had evidently been coming upon him.

The place called the cuddy was a light deck-cabin formed by the poop,
a sort of attic to the large cabin below. Part of it had formerly been the quarters of the officers; but since their death all the partitionings had been
thrown down, and the whole interior converted into one spacious and airy
marine hall; for absence of fine furniture and picturesque disarray, of odd
appurtenances, somewhat answering to the wide, cluttered hall of some
eccentric bachelor-squire in the country, who hangs his shooting-jacket

and tobacco-pouch on deer antlers, and keeps his fishing-rod, tongs, and walking-stick in the same corner.

The similitude was heightened, if not originally suggested, by glimpses of the surrounding sea; since, in one aspect, the country and the ocean seem cousins-german.

The floor of the cuddy was matted. Overhead, four or five old muskets were stuck into horizontal holes along the beams. On one side was a claw-footed old table lashed to the deck; a thumbed missal on it, and over it a small, meager crucifix attached to the bulk-head. Under the table lay a dented cutlass or two, with a hacked harpoon, among some melancholy old rigging, like a heap of poor friar's girdles. There were also two long, sharp-ribbed settees of malacca cane, black with age, and uncomfortable to look at as inquisitors' racks, with a large, misshapen arm-chair, which, furnished with a rude barber's crutch at the back, working with a screw, seemed some grotesque, middle-age[21] engine of torment. A flag locker was in one corner, open, exposing various colored bunting, some rolled up, others half unrolled, still others tumbled. Opposite was a cumbrous washstand, of black mahogany, all of one block, with a pedestal, like a font, and over it a railed shelf, containing combs, brushes, and other implements of the toilet. A torn hammock of stained grass swung near; the sheets tossed, and the pillow wrinkled up like a brow, as if whoever slept here slept but illy, with alternate visitations of sad thoughts and bad dreams.

The further extremity of the cuddy, overhanging the ship's stern, was pierced with three openings, windows or port holes, according as men or cannon might peer, socially or unsocially, out of them. At present neither men nor cannon were seen, though huge ring-bolts and other rusty iron fixtures of the wood-work hinted of twenty-four-pounders.

Glancing towards the hammock as he entered, Captain Delano said, "You sleep here, Don Benito?"

"Yes, Señor, since we got into mild weather."

"This seems a sort of dormitory, sitting-room, sail-loft, chapel, armory, and private closet all together, Don Benito," added Captain Delano, looking round.

"Yes, Señor; events have not been favorable to much order in my arrangements."

---

21. *middle-age*: Medieval. The imagery in this paragraph suggests Inquisitorial violence against heretics, Moors (black Africans), and Jews in medieval and Renaissance Spain.

Here the servant, napkin on arm, made a motion as if waiting his master's good pleasure. Don Benito signified his readiness, when, seating him in the malacca arm-chair, and for the guest's convenience drawing opposite it one of the settees, the servant commenced operations by throwing back his master's collar and loosening his cravat.

There is something in the negro which, in a peculiar way, fits him for avocations about one's person. Most negroes are natural valets and hairdressers; taking to the comb and brush congenially as to the castinets, and flourishing them apparently with almost equal satisfaction. There is, too, a smooth tact about them in this employment, with a marvelous, noiseless, gliding briskness, not ungraceful in its way, singularly pleasing to behold, and still more so to be the manipulated subject of. And above all is the great gift of good humor. Not the mere grin or laugh is here meant. Those were unsuitable. But a certain easy cheerfulness, harmonious in every glance and gesture; as though God had set the whole negro to some pleasant tune.

When to all this is added the docility arising from the unaspiring contentment of a limited mind, and that susceptibility of blind attachment sometimes inhering in indisputable inferiors, one readily perceives why those hypochondriacs, Johnson and Byron – it may be something like the hypochondriac, Benito Cereno – took to their hearts, almost to the exclusion of the entire white race, their serving men, the negroes, Barber and Fletcher.[22] But if there be that in the negro which exempts him from the inflicted sourness of the morbid or cynical mind, how, in his most prepossessing aspects, must he appear to a benevolent one? When at ease with respect to exterior things, Captain Delano's nature was not only benign, but familiarly and humorously so. At home, he had often taken rare satisfaction in sitting in his door, watching some free man of color at his work or play. If on a voyage he chanced to have a black sailor, invariably he was on chatty, and half-gamesome terms with him. In fact, like most men of a good, blithe heart, Captain Delano took to negroes, not philanthropically, but genially, just as other men to Newfoundland dogs.

Hitherto the circumstances in which he found the San Dominick had repressed the tendency. But in the cuddy, relieved from his former uneasiness, and, for various reasons, more sociably inclined than at any previous period of the day, and seeing the colored servant, napkin on arm, so debonair

---

22. *Barber and Fletcher:* Francis Barber was the African servant of the English author Samuel Johnson (1709-1784). Melville may be confusing William Fletcher, a white valet of Lord Byron (1788-1824), with another black servant.

about his master, in a business so familiar as that of shaving, too, all his old weakness for negroes returned.

Among other things, he was amused with an odd instance of the African love of bright colors and fine shows, in the black's informally taking from the flag-locker a great piece of bunting of all hues, and lavishly tucking it under his master's chin for an apron.

The mode of shaving among the Spaniards is a little different from what it is with other nations. They have a basin, specifically called a barber's basin, which on one side is scooped out, so as accurately to receive the chin, against which it is closely held in lathering; which is done, not with a brush, but with soap dipped in the water of the basin and rubbed on the face.

In the present instance salt-water was used for lack of better; and the parts lathered were only the upper lip, and low down under the throat, all the rest being cultivated beard.

The preliminaries being somewhat novel to Captain Delano, he sat curiously eying them, so that no conversation took place, nor for the present did Don Benito appear disposed to renew any.

Setting down his basin, the negro searched among the razors, as for the sharpest, and having found it, gave it an additional edge by expertly strapping it on the firm, smooth, oily skin of his open palm; he then made a gesture as if to begin, but midway stood suspended for an instant, one hand elevating the razor, the other professionally dabbling among the bubbling suds on the Spaniard's lank neck. Not unaffected by the close sight of the gleaming steel, Don Benito nervously shuddered; his usual ghastliness was heightened by the lather, which lather, again, was intensified in its hue by the contrasting sootiness of the negro's body. Altogether the scene was somewhat peculiar, at least to Captain Delano, nor, as he saw the two thus postured, could he resist the vagary, that in the black he saw a headsman, and in the white, a man at the block. But this was one of those antic conceits, appearing and vanishing in a breath, from which, perhaps, the best regulated mind is not always free.

Meantime the agitation of the Spaniard had a little loosened the bunting from around him, so that one broad fold swept curtain-like over the chair-arm to the floor, revealing, amid a profusion of armorial bars and ground-colors – black, blue, and yellow – a closed castle in a blood-red field diagonal with a lion rampant in a white.

"The castle and the lion," exclaimed Captain Delano – "why, Don Benito, this is the flag of Spain you use here. It's well it's only I, and not the King, that sees this," he added with a smile, "but" – turning towards the black, – "it's all one, I suppose, so the colors be gay"; which playful remark did not fail somewhat to tickle the negro.

"Now, master," he said, readjusting the flag, and pressing the head gently further back into the crotch of the chair; "now master," and the steel glanced nigh the throat.

Again Don Benito faintly shuddered.

"You must not shake so, master. – See, Don Amasa, master always shakes when I shave him. And yet master knows I never yet have drawn blood, though it's true, if master will shake so, I may some of these times. Now master," he continued. "And now, Don Amasa, please go on with your talk about the gale, and all that, master can hear, and between times master can answer."

"Ah yes, these gales," said Captain Delano; "but the more I think of your voyage, Don Benito, the more I wonder, not at the gales, terrible as they must have been, but at the disastrous interval following them. For here, by your account, have you been these two months and more getting from Cape Horn to St. Maria, a distance which I myself, with a good wind, have sailed in a few days. True, you had calms, and long ones, but to be becalmed for two months, that is, at least, unusual. Why, Don Benito, had almost any other gentleman told me such a story, I should have been half disposed to a little incredulity."

Here an involuntary expression came over the Spaniard, similar to that just before on the deck, and whether it was the start he gave, or a sudden gawky roll of the hull in the calm, or a momentary unsteadiness of the servant's hand; however it was, just then the razor drew blood, spots of which stained the creamy lather under the throat; immediately the black barber drew back his steel, and remaining in his professional attitude, back to Captain Delano, and face to Don Benito, held up the trickling razor, saying, with a sort of half humorous sorrow, "See, master, – you shook so – here's Babo's first blood."

No sword drawn before James the First of England,[23] no assassination in that timid King's presence, could have produced a more terrified aspect than was now presented by Don Benito.

Poor fellow, thought Captain Delano, so nervous he can't even bear the sight of barber's blood; and this unstrung, sick man, is it credible that I should have imagined he meant to spill all my blood, who can't endure the sight of one little drop of his own? Surely, Amasa Delano, you have been beside yourself this day. Tell it not when you get home, sappy Amasa. Well, well, he looks like a murderer, doesn't he? More like as if himself were to be done for. Well, well, this day's experience shall be a good lesson.

---

23. *James the First of England:* The king against whom Guy Fawkes and his party planned the Gunpowder Plot.

Meantime, while these things were running through the honest seaman's mind, the servant had taken the napkin from his arm, and to Don Benito had said – "But answer Don Amasa, please, master, while I wipe this ugly stuff off the razor, and strop it again."

As he said the words, his face was turned half round, so as to be alike visible to the Spaniard and the American, and seemed by its expression to hint, that he was desirous, by getting his master to go on with the conversation, considerately to withdraw his attention from the recent annoying accident. As if glad to snatch the offered relief, Don Benito resumed, rehearsing to Captain Delano, that not only were the calms of unusual duration, but the ship had fallen in with obstinate currents; and other things he added, some of which were but repetitions of former statements, to explain how it came to pass that the passage from Cape Horn to St. Maria had been so exceedingly long, now and then mingling with his words, incidental praises, less qualified than before, to the blacks, for their general good conduct.

These particulars were not given consecutively, the servant, at convenient times, using his razor, and so, between the intervals of shaving, the story and panegyric went on with more than usual huskiness.

To Captain Delano's imagination, now again not wholly at rest, there was something so hollow in the Spaniard's manner, with apparently some reciprocal hollowness in the servant's dusky comment of silence, that the idea flashed across him, that possibly master and man, for some unknown purpose, were acting out, both in word and deed, nay, to the very tremor of Don Benito's limbs, some juggling play before him. Neither did the suspicion of collusion lack apparent support, from the fact of those whispered conferences before mentioned. But then, what could be the object of enacting this play of the barber before him? At last, regarding the notion as a whimsy, insensibly suggested, perhaps, by the theatrical aspect of Don Benito in his harlequin ensign, Captain Delano speedily banished it.

The shaving over, the servant bestirred himself with a small bottle of scented waters, pouring a few drops on the head, and then diligently rubbing; the vehemence of the exercise causing the muscles of his face to twitch rather strangely.

His next operation was with comb, scissors and brush; going round and round, smoothing a curl here, clipping an unruly whisker-hair there, giving a graceful sweep to the temple-lock, with other impromptu touches evincing the hand of a master; while, like any resigned gentleman in barber's hands, Don Benito bore all, much less uneasily, at least, than he had done the razoring; indeed, he sat so pale and rigid now, that the negro seemed a Nubian sculptor finishing off a white statue-head.

All being over at last, the standard of Spain removed, tumbled up, and tossed back into the flag-locker, the negro's warm breath blowing away any stray hair which might have lodged down his master's neck; collar and cravat readjusted; a speck of lint whisked off the velvet lapel; all this being done; backing off a little space, and pausing with an expression of subdued self-complacency, the servant for a moment surveyed his master, as, in toilet at least, the creature of his own tasteful hands.

Captain Delano playfully complimented him upon his achievement; at the same time congratulating Don Benito.

But neither sweet waters, nor shampooing, nor fidelity, nor sociality, delighted the Spaniard. Seeing him relapsing into forbidding gloom, and still remaining seated, Captain Delano, thinking that his presence was undesired just then, withdrew, on pretense of seeing whether, as he had prophecied, any signs of a breeze were visible.

Walking forward to the mainmast, he stood awhile thinking over the scene, and not without some undefined misgivings, when he heard a noise near the cuddy, and turning, saw the negro, his hand to his cheek. Advancing, Captain Delano perceived that the cheek was bleeding. He was about to ask the cause, when the negro's wailing soliloquy enlightened him.

"Ah, when will master get better from his sickness; only the sour heart that sour sickness breeds made him serve Babo so; cutting Babo with the razor, because, only by accident, Babo had given master one little scratch; and for the first time in so many a day, too. Ah, ah, ah," holding his hand to his face.

Is it possible, thought Captain Delano; was it to wreak in private his Spanish spite against this poor friend of his, that Don Benito, by his sullen manner, impelled me to withdraw? Ah, this slavery breeds ugly passions in man. – Poor fellow!

He was about to speak in sympathy to the negro, but with a timid reluctance he now reëntered the cuddy.

Presently master and man came forth; Don Benito leaning on his servant as if nothing had happened.

But a sort of love-quarrel, after all, thought Captain Delano.

He accosted Don Benito, and they slowly walked together. They had gone but a few paces, when the steward – a tall, rajah-looking mulatto, orientally set off with a pagoda turban formed by three or four Madras handkerchiefs wound about his head, tier on tier – approaching with a salaam, announced lunch in the cabin.

On their way thither, the two Captains were preceded by the mulatto, who, turning round as he advanced, with continual smiles and bows, ushered them on, a display of elegance which quite completed the insignificance of the small bare-headed Babo, who, as if not unconscious of inferiority, eyed askance the graceful steward. But in part, Captain Delano imputed his jealous watchfulness to that peculiar feeling which the full-blooded African entertains for the adulterated one. As for the steward, his manner, if not bespeaking much dignity of self-respect, yet evidenced his extreme desire to please: which is doubly meritorious, as at once Christian and Chesterfieldian.[24]

Captain Delano observed with interest that while the complexion of the mulatto was hybrid, his physiognomy was European; classically so.

"Don Benito," whispered he, "I am glad to see this usher-of-the-golden-rod of yours; the sight refutes an ugly remark once made to me by a Barbadoes planter; that when a mulatto has a regular European face, look out for him; he is a devil. But see, your steward here has features more regular than King George's of England; and yet there he nods, and bows, and smiles; a king, indeed – the king of kind hearts and polite fellows. What a pleasant voice he has, too!"

"He has, Señor."

"But, tell me, has he not, so far as you have known him, always proved a good, worthy fellow?" said Captain Delano, pausing, while with a final genuflexion the steward disappeared into the cabin; "come, for the reason just mentioned, I am curious to know."

"Francesco is a good man," a sort of sluggishly responded Don Benito, like a phlegmatic appreciator, who would neither find fault nor flatter.

"Ah, I thought so. For it were strange indeed, and not very creditable to us white-skins, if a little of our blood mixed with the African's should, far from improving the latter's quality, have the sad effect of pouring vitriolic acid into black broth; improving the hue, perhaps, but not the wholesomeness."

"Doubtless, doubtless, Señor, but" – glancing at Babo – "not to speak of negroes, your planter's remark I have heard applied to the Spanish and Indian intermixtures in our provinces. But I know nothing about the matter," he listlessly added.

And here they entered the cabin.

The lunch was a frugal one. Some of Captain Delano's fresh fish and pumpkins, biscuit and salt beef, the reserved bottle of cider, and the San Dominick's last bottle of Canary.

---

24. *Chesterfieldian:* Referring to Philip Stanhope, Earl of Chesterfield (1694–1773), whose letters to his son provided an expedient model of social behavior and a polished alternative to Christian morality.

As they entered, Francesco, with two or three colored aids, was hovering over the table giving the last adjustments. Upon perceiving their master they withdrew, Francesco making a smiling congé, and the Spaniard, without condescending to notice it, fastidiously remarking to his companion that he relished not superfluous attendance.

Without companions, host and guest sat down, like a childless married couple, at opposite ends of the table, Don Benito waving Captain Delano to his place, and, weak as he was, insisting upon that gentleman being seated before himself.

The negro placed a rug under Don Benito's feet, and a cushion behind his back, and then stood behind, not his master's chair, but Captain Delano's. At first, this a little surprised the latter. But it was soon evident that, in taking his position, the black was still true to his master; since by facing him he could the more readily anticipate his slightest want.

"This is an uncommonly intelligent fellow of yours, Don Benito," whispered Captain Delano across the table.

"You say true, Señor."

During the repast, the guest again reverted to parts of Don Benito's story, begging further particulars here and there. He inquired how it was that the scurvy and fever should have committed such wholesale havoc upon the whites, while destroying less than half of the blacks. As if this question reproduced the whole scene of plague before the Spaniard's eyes, miserably reminding him of his solitude in a cabin where before he had had so many friends and officers round him, his hand shook, his face became hueless, broken words escaped; but directly the sane memory of the past seemed replaced by insane terrors of the present. With starting eyes he stared before him at vacancy. For nothing was to be seen but the hand of his servant pushing the Canary over towards him. At length a few sips served partially to restore him. He made random reference to the different constitution of races, enabling one to offer more resistance to certain maladies than another. The thought was new to his companion. *Scurvy?*

Presently Captain Delano, intending to say something to his host concerning the pecuniary part of the business he had undertaken for him, especially – since he was strictly accountable to his owners – with reference to the new suit of sails, and other things of that sort; and naturally preferring to conduct such affairs in private, was desirous that the servant should withdraw; imagining that Don Benito for a few minutes could dispense with his attendance. He, however, waited awhile; thinking that, as the conversation proceeded, Don Benito, without being prompted, would perceive the propriety of the step.

But it was otherwise. At last catching his host's eye, Captain Delano, with a slight backward gesture of his thumb, whispered, "Don Benito, pardon me, but there is an interference with the full expression of what I have to say to you."

Upon this the Spaniard changed countenance; which was imputed to his resenting the hint, as in some way a reflection upon his servant. After a moment's pause, he assured his guest that the black's remaining with them could be of no disservice; because since losing his officers he had made Babo (whose original office, it now appeared, had been captain of the slaves) not only his constant attendant and companion, but in all things his confidant.

After this, nothing more could be said; though, indeed, Captain Delano could hardly avoid some little tinge of irritation upon being left ungratified in so inconsiderable a wish, by one, too, for whom he intended such solid services. But it is only his querulousness, thought he; and so filling his glass he proceeded to business.

The price of the sails and other matters was fixed upon. But while this was being done, the American observed that, though his original offer of assistance had been hailed with hectic animation, yet now when it was reduced to a business transaction, indifference and apathy were betrayed. Don Benito, in fact, appeared to submit to hearing the details more out of regard to common propriety, than from any impression that weighty benefit to himself and his voyage was involved.

Soon, this manner became still more reserved. The effort was vain to seek to draw him into social talk. Gnawed by his splenetic mood, he sat twitching his beard, while to little purpose the hand of his servant, mute as that on the wall, slowly pushed over the Canary.

Lunch being over, they sat down on the cushioned transom; the servant placing a pillow behind his master. The long continuance of the calm had now affected the atmosphere. Don Benito sighed heavily, as if for breath.

"Why not adjourn to the cuddy," said Captain Delano; "there is more air there." But the host sat silent and motionless.

Meantime his servant knelt before him, with a large fan of feathers. And Francesco coming in on tiptoes, handed the negro a little cup of aromatic waters, with which at intervals he chafed his master's brow; smoothing the hair along the temples as a nurse does a child's. He spoke no word. He only rested his eye on his master's, as if, amid all Don Benito's distress, a little to refresh his spirit by the silent sight of fidelity.

Presently the ship's bell sounded two o'clock; and through the cabin-windows a slight rippling of the sea was discerned; and from the desired direction.

"There," exclaimed Captain Delano, "I told you so, Don Benito, look!" He had risen to his feet, speaking in a very animated tone, with a view the more to rouse his companion. But though the crimson curtain of the stern-window near him that moment fluttered against his pale cheek, Don Benito seemed to have even less welcome for the breeze than the calm.

Poor fellow, thought Captain Delano, bitter experience has taught him that one ripple does not make a wind, any more than one swallow a summer. But he is mistaken for once. I will get his ship in for him, and prove it.

Briefly alluding to his weak condition, he urged his host to remain quietly where he was, since he (Captain Delano) would with pleasure take upon himself the responsibility of making the best use of the wind.

Upon gaining the deck, Captain Delano started at the unexpected figure of Atufal, monumentally fixed at the threshold, like one of those sculptured porters of black marble guarding the porches of Egyptian tombs.

But this time the start was, perhaps, purely physical. Atufal's presence, singularly attesting docility even in sullenness, was contrasted with that of the hatchet-polishers, who in patience evinced their industry; while both spectacles showed, that lax as Don Benito's general authority might be, still, whenever he chose to exert it, no man so savage or colossal but must, more or less, bow.

Snatching a trumpet which hung from the bulwarks, with a free step Captain Delano advanced to the forward edge of the poop, issuing his orders in his best Spanish. The few sailors and many negroes, all equally pleased, obediently set about heading the ship towards the harbor.

While giving some directions about setting a lower stu'n'-sail, suddenly Captain Delano heard a voice faithfully repeating his orders. Turning, he saw Babo, now for the time acting, under the pilot, his original part of captain of the slaves. This assistance proved valuable. Tattered sails and warped yards were soon brought into some trim. And no brace or halyard was pulled but to the blithe songs of the inspirited negroes.

Good fellows, thought Captain Delano, a little training would make fine sailors of them. Why see, the very women pull and sing too. These must be some of those Ashantee negresses that make such capital soldiers, I've heard. But who's at the helm. I must have a good hand there.

He went to see.

The San Dominick steered with a cumbrous tiller, with large horizontal pullies attached. At each pully-end stood a subordinate black, and between them, at the tiller-head, the responsible post, a Spanish seaman, whose countenance evinced his due share in the general hopefulness and confidence at the coming of the breeze.

He proved the same man who had behaved with so shame-faced an air on the windlass.

"Ah, – it is you, man," exclaimed Captain Delano – "well, no more sheep's-eyes now; – look straight forward and keep the ship so. Good hand, I trust? And want to get into the harbor, don't you?"

The man assented with an inward chuckle, grasping the tiller-head firmly. Upon this, unperceived by the American, the two blacks eyed the sailor intently.

Finding all right at the helm, the pilot went forward to the forecastle, to see how matters stood there.

The ship now had way enough to breast the current. With the approach of evening, the breeze would be sure to freshen.

Having done all that was needed for the present, Captain Delano, giving his last orders to the sailors, turned aft to report affairs to Don Benito in the cabin; perhaps additionally incited to rejoin him by the hope of snatching a moment's private chat while his servant was engaged upon deck.

From opposite sides, there were, beneath the poop, two approaches to the cabin; one further forward than the other, and consequently communicating with a longer passage. Marking the servant still above, Captain Delano, taking the nighest entrance – the one last named, and at whose porch Atufal still stood – hurried on his way, till, arrived at the cabin threshold, he paused an instant, a little to recover from his eagerness. Then, with the words of his intended business upon his lips, he entered. As he advanced toward the seated Spaniard, he heard another footstep, keeping time with his. From the opposite door, a salver in hand, the servant was likewise advancing.

"Confound the faithful fellow," thought Captain Delano; "what a vexatious coincidence."

Possibly, the vexation might have been something different, were it not for the brisk confidence inspired by the breeze. But even as it was, he felt a slight twinge, from a sudden indefinite association in his mind of Babo with Atufal.

"Don Benito," said he, "I give you joy; the breeze will hold, and will increase. By the way, your tall man and time-piece, Atufal, stands without. By your order, of course?"

Don Benito recoiled, as if at some bland satirical touch, delivered with such adroit garnish of apparent good-breeding as to present no handle for retort.

He is like one flayed alive, thought Captain Delano; where may one touch him without causing a shrink?

The servant moved before his master, adjusting a cushion; recalled to civility, the Spaniard stiffly replied: "You are right. The slave appears where you saw him, according to my command; which is, that if at the given hour I am below, he must take his stand and abide my coming."

"Ah now, pardon me, but that is treating the poor fellow like an ex-king indeed. Ah, Don Benito," smiling, "for all the license you permit in some things, I fear lest, at bottom, you are a bitter hard master."

Again Don Benito shrank; and this time, as the good sailor thought, from a genuine twinge of his conscience.

Again conversation became constrained. In vain Captain Delano called attention to the now perceptible motion of the keel gently cleaving the sea; with lack-lustre eye, Don Benito returned words few and reserved.

By-and-by, the wind having steadily risen, and still blowing right into the harbor, bore the San Dominick swiftly on. Rounding a point of land, the sealer at distance came into open view.

Meantime Captain Delano had again repaired to the deck, remaining there some time. Having at last altered the ship's course, so as to give the reef a wide berth, he returned for a few moments below.

I will cheer up my poor friend, this time, thought he.

"Better and better, Don Benito," he cried as he blithely reëntered; "there will soon be an end to your cares, at least for awhile. For when, after a long, sad voyage, you know, the anchor drops into the haven, all its vast weight seems lifted from the captain's heart. We are getting on famously, Don Benito. My ship is in sight. Look through this side-light here; there she is; all a-taunt-o! The Bachelor's Delight, my good friend. Ah, how this wind braces one up. Come, you must take a cup of coffee with me this evening. My old steward will give you as fine a cup as ever any sultan tasted. What say you, Don Benito, will you?"

At first, the Spaniard glanced feverishly up, casting a longing look towards the sealer, while with mute concern his servant gazed into his face. Suddenly the old ague of coldness returned, and dropping back to his cushions he was silent.

"You do not answer. Come, all day you have been my host; would you have hospitality all on one side?"

"I cannot go," was the response.

"What? it will not fatigue you. The ships will lie together as near as they can, without swinging foul. It will be little more than stepping from deck to deck; which is but as from room to room. Come, come, you must not refuse me."

"I cannot go," decisively and repulsively repeated Don Benito.

Renouncing all but the last appearance of courtesy, with a sort of cadaverous sullenness, and biting his thin nails to the quick, he glanced, almost glared, at his guest; as if impatient that a stranger's presence should interfere with the full indulgence of his morbid hour. Meantime the sound of the parted waters came more and more gurglingly and merrily in at the windows; as reproaching him for his dark spleen; as telling him that, sulk as he might, and go mad with it, nature cared not a jot; since, whose fault was it, pray?

But the foul mood was now at its depth, as the fair wind at its height.

There was something in the man so far beyond any mere unsociality or sourness previously evinced, that even the forbearing good-nature of his guest could no longer endure it. Wholly at a loss to account for such demeanor, and deeming sickness with eccentricity, however extreme, no adequate excuse, well satisfied, too, that nothing in his own conduct could justify it, Captain Delano's pride began to be roused. Himself became reserved. But all seemed one to the Spaniard. Quitting him, therefore, Captain Delano once more went to the deck.

The ship was now within less than two miles of the sealer. The whaleboat was seen darting over the interval.

To be brief, the two vessels, thanks to the pilot's skill, ere long in neighborly style lay anchored together.

Before returning to his own vessel, Captain Delano had intended communicating to Don Benito the smaller details of the proposed services to be rendered. But, as it was, unwilling anew to subject himself to rebuffs, he resolved, now that he had seen the San Dominick safely moored, immediately to quit her, without further allusion to hospitality or business. Indefinitely postponing his ulterior plans, he would regulate his future actions according to future circumstances. His boat was ready to receive him; but his host still tarried below. Well, thought Captain Delano, if he has little breeding, the more need to show mine. He descended to the cabin to bid a ceremonious, and, it may be, tacitly rebukeful adieu. But to his great satisfaction, Don Benito, as if he began to feel the weight of that treatment with which his slighted guest had, not indecorously, retaliated upon him, now supported by his servant, rose to his feet, and grasping Captain Delano's hand, stood tremulous; too much agitated to speak. But the good augury hence drawn was suddenly dashed, by his resuming all his previous reserve, with augmented gloom, as, with half-averted eyes, he silently reseated himself on his cushions. With a corresponding return of his own chilled feelings, Captain Delano bowed and withdrew.

He was hardly midway in the narrow corridor, dim as a tunnel, leading from the cabin to the stairs, when a sound, as of the tolling for execution in some jail-yard, fell on his ears. It was the echo of the ship's flawed bell, striking the hour, drearily reverberated in this subterranean vault. Instantly, by a fatality not to be withstood, his mind, responsive to the portent, swarmed with superstitious suspicions. He paused. In images far swifter than these sentences, the minutest details of all his former distrusts swept through him.

Hitherto, credulous good-nature had been too ready to furnish excuses for reasonable fears. Why was the Spaniard, so superfluously punctilious at times, now heedless of common propriety in not accompanying to the side his departing guest? Did indisposition forbid? Indisposition had not forbidden more irksome exertion that day. His last equivocal demeanor recurred. He had risen to his feet, grasped his guest's hand, motioned toward his hat; then, in an instant, all was eclipsed in sinister muteness and gloom. Did this imply one brief, repentent [*sic*] relenting at the final moment, from some iniquitous plot, followed by remorseless return to it? His last glance seemed to express a calamitous, yet acquiescent farewell to Captain Delano forever. Why decline the invitation to visit the sealer that evening? Or was the Spaniard less hardened than the Jew,[25] who refrained not from supping at the board of him whom the same night he meant to betray? What imported all those day-long enigmas and contradictions, except they were intended to mystify, preliminary to some stealthy blow? Atufal, the pretended rebel, but punctual shadow, that moment lurked by the threshold without. He seemed a sentry, and more. Who, by his own confession, had stationed him there? Was the negro now lying in wait?

The Spaniard behind – his creature before: to rush from darkness to light was the involuntary choice.

The next moment, with clenched jaw and hand, he passed Atufal, and stood unharmed in the light. As he saw his trim ship lying peacefully at her anchor, and almost within ordinary call; as he saw his household boat, with familiar faces in it, patiently rising and falling on the short waves by the San Dominick's side; and then, glancing about the decks where he stood, saw the oakum-pickers still gravely plying their fingers; and heard the low, buzzing whistle and industrious hum of the hatchet-polishers, still bestirring themselves over their endless occupation; and more than all, as he saw the benign aspect of nature, taking her innocent repose in the evening; the screened sun in the quiet camp of the west shining out like the mild light from Abraham's tent; as charmed eye and ear took in all

25. *the Jew:* Judas Iscariot, who betrayed Jesus after the Last Supper.

these, with the chained figure of the black, clenched jaw and hand relaxed. Once again he smiled at the phantoms which had mocked him, and felt something like a tinge of remorse, that, by harboring them even for a moment, he should, by implication, have betrayed an almost atheist doubt of the ever-watchful Providence above.

There was a few minutes' delay, while, in obedience to his orders, the boat was being hooked along to the gangway. During this interval, a sort of saddened satisfaction stole over Captain Delano, at thinking of the kindly offices he had that day discharged for a stranger. Ah, thought he, after good actions one's conscience is never ungrateful, however much so the benefited party may be.

Presently, his foot, in the first act of descent into the boat, pressed the first round of the side-ladder, his face presented inward upon the deck. In the same moment, he heard his name courteously sounded; and, to his pleased surprise, saw Don Benito advancing – an unwonted energy in his air, as if, at the last moment, intent upon making amends for his recent discourtesy. With instinctive good feeling, Captain Delano, withdrawing his foot, turned and reciprocally advanced. As he did so, the Spaniard's nervous eagerness increased, but his vital energy failed; so that, the better to support him, the servant, placing his master's hand on his naked shoulder, and gently holding it there, formed himself into a sort of crutch.

When the two captains met, the Spaniard again fervently took the hand of the American, at the same time casting an earnest glance into his eyes, but, as before, too much overcome to speak.

I have done him wrong, self-reproachfully thought Captain Delano; his apparent coldness has deceived me; in no instance has he meant to offend.

Meantime, as if fearful that the continuance of the scene might too much unstring his master, the servant seemed anxious to terminate it. And so, still presenting himself as a crutch, and walking between the two captains, he advanced with them towards the gangway; while still, as if full of kindly contrition, Don Benito would not let go the hand of Captain Delano, but retained it in his, across the black's body.

Soon they were standing by the side, looking over into the boat, whose crew turned up their curious eyes. Waiting a moment for the Spaniard to relinquish his hold, the now embarrassed Captain Delano lifted his foot, to overstep the threshold of the open gangway; but still Don Benito would not let go his hand. And yet, with an agitated tone, he said, "I can go no further; here I must bid you adieu. Adieu, my dear, dear Don Amasa. Go – go!" suddenly tearing his hand loose, "go, and God guard you better than me, my best friend."

Not unaffected, Captain Delano would now have lingered; but catching the meekly admonitory eye of the servant, with a hasty farewell he descended into his boat, followed by the continual adieus of Don Benito, standing rooted in the gangway.

Seating himself in the stern, Captain Delano, making a last salute, ordered the boat shoved off. The crew had their oars on end. The bowsman pushed the boat a sufficient distance for the oars to be lengthwise dropped. The instant that was done, Don Benito sprang over the bulwarks, falling at the feet of Captain Delano; at the same time, calling towards his ship, but in tones so frenzied, that none in the boat could understand him. But, as if not equally obtuse, three sailors, from three different and distant parts of the ship, splashed into the sea, swimming after their captain, as if intent upon his rescue.

The dismayed officer of the boat eagerly asked what this meant. To which, Captain Delano, turning a disdainful smile upon the unaccountable Spaniard, answered that, for his part, he neither knew nor cared; but it seemed as if Don Benito had taken it into his head to produce the impression among his people that the boat wanted to kidnap him. "Or else – give way for your lives," he wildly added, starting at a clottering hubbub in the ship, above which rang the tocsin of the hatchet-polishers; and seizing Don Benito by the throat he added, "this plotting pirate means murder!" Here, in apparent verification of the words, the servant, a dagger in his hand, was seen on the rail overhead, poised, in the act of leaping, as if with desperate fidelity to befriend his master to the last; while, seemingly to aid the black, the three white sailors were trying to clamber into the hampered bow. Meantime, the whole host of negroes, as if inflamed at the sight of their jeopardized captain, impended in one sooty avalanche over the bulwarks.

All this, with what preceded, and what followed, occurred with such involutions of rapidity, that past, present, and future seemed one.

Seeing the negro coming, Captain Delano had flung the Spaniard aside, almost in the very act of clutching him, and, by the unconscious recoil, shifting his place, with arms thrown up, so promptly grappled the servant in his descent, that with dagger presented at Captain Delano's heart, the black seemed of purpose to have leaped there as to his mark. But the weapon was wrenched away, and the assailant dashed down into the bottom of the boat, which now, with disentangled oars, began to speed through the sea.

At this juncture, the left hand of Captain Delano, on one side, again clutched the half-reclined Don Benito, heedless that he was in a speechless faint, while his right foot, on the other side, ground the prostrate negro;

and his right arm pressed for added speed on the after oar, his eye bent forward, encouraging his men to their utmost.

But here, the officer of the boat, who had at last succeeded in beating off the towing sailors, and was now, with face turned aft, assisting the bowsman at his oar, suddenly called to Captain Delano, to see what the black was about; while a Portuguese oarsman shouted to him to give heed to what the Spaniard was saying.

Glancing down at his feet, Captain Delano saw the freed hand of the servant aiming with a second dagger – a small one, before concealed in his wool – with this he was snakishly writhing up from the boat's bottom, at the heart of his master, his countenance lividly vindictive, expressing the centred purpose of his soul; while the Spaniard, half-choked, was vainly shrinking away, with husky words, incoherent to all but the Portuguese.

That moment, across the long-benighted mind of Captain Delano, a flash of revelation swept, illuminating in unanticipated clearness his host's whole mysterious demeanor, with every enigmatic event of the day, as well as the entire past voyage of the San Dominick. He smote Babo's hand down, but his own heart smote him harder. With infinite pity he withdrew his hold from Don Benito. Not Captain Delano, but Don Benito, the black, in leaping into the boat, had intended to stab.

Both the black's hands were held, as, glancing up towards the San Dominick, Captain Delano, now with the scales dropped from his eyes, saw the negroes, not in misrule, not in tumult, not as if frantically concerned for Don Benito, but with mask torn away, flourishing hatchets and knives, in ferocious piratical revolt. Like delirious black dervishes, the six Ashantees danced on the poop. Prevented by their foes from springing into the water, the Spanish boys were hurrying up to the topmost spars, while such of the few Spanish sailors, not already in the sea, less alert, were descried, helplessly mixed in, on deck, with the blacks.

Meantime Captain Delano hailed his own vessel, ordering the ports up, and the guns run out. But by this time the cable of the San Dominick had been cut; and the fag-end, in lashing out, whipped away the canvas shroud about the beak, suddenly revealing, as the bleached hull swung round towards the open ocean, death for the figure-head, in a human skeleton; chalky comment on the chalked words below, *"Follow your leader."*

At the sight, Don Benito, covering his face, wailed out: "'Tis he, Aranda! my murdered, unburied friend!"

Upon reaching the sealer, calling for ropes, Captain Delano bound the negro, who made no resistance, and had him hoisted to the deck. He would then have assisted the now almost helpless Don Benito up the side; but Don Benito, wan as he was, refused to move, or be moved, until the negro should have been first put below out of view. When, presently assured that it was done, he no more shrank from the ascent.

The boat was immediately dispatched back to pick up the three swimming sailors. Meantime, the guns were in readiness, though, owing to the San Dominick having glided somewhat astern of the sealer, only the aftermost one could be brought to bear. With this, they fired six times; thinking to cripple the fugitive ship by bringing down her spars. But only a few inconsiderable ropes were shot away. Soon the ship was beyond the gun's range, steering broad out of the bay; the blacks thickly clustering round the bowsprit, one moment with taunting cries towards the whites, the next with upthrown gestures hailing the now dusky moors of ocean – cawing crows escaped from the hand of the fowler.

The first impulse was to slip the cables and give chase. But, upon second thoughts, to pursue with whale-boat and yawl seemed more promising.

Upon inquiring of Don Benito what fire arms they had on board the San Dominick, Captain Delano was answered that they had none that could be used; because, in the earlier stages of the mutiny, a cabin-passenger, since dead, had secretly put out of order the locks of what few muskets there were. But with all his remaining strength, Don Benito entreated the American not to give chase, either with ship or boat; for the negroes had already proved themselves such desperadoes, that, in case of a present assault, nothing but a total massacre of the whites could be looked for. But, regarding this warning as coming from one whose spirit had been crushed by misery, the American did not give up his design.

The boats were got ready and armed. Captain Delano ordered his men into them. He was going himself when Don Benito grasped his arm.

"What! have you saved my life, señor, and are you now going to throw away your own?"

The officers also, for reasons connected with their interests and those of the voyage, and a duty owing to the owners, strongly objected against their commander's going. Weighing their remonstrances a moment, Captain Delano felt bound to remain; appointing his chief mate – an athletic and resolute man, who had been a privateer's-man, and, as his enemies whispered, a pirate – to head the party. The more to encourage the sailors, they were told, that the Spanish captain considered his ship as good as lost; that she and her cargo, including some gold and silver, were worth more than a thousand doubloons. Take her, and no small part should be theirs. The sailors replied with a shout.

The fugitives had now almost gained an offing. It was nearly night; but the moon was rising. After hard, prolonged pulling, the boats came up on the ship's quarters, at a suitable distance laying upon their oars to discharge their muskets. Having no bullets to return, the negroes sent their yells. But, upon the second volley, Indian-like, they hurtled their hatchets. One took off a sailor's fingers. Another struck the whale-boat's bow, cutting off the rope there, and remaining stuck in the gunwale like a woodman's axe. Snatching it, quivering from its lodgment, the mate hurled it back. The returned gauntlet now stuck in the ship's broken quarter-gallery, and so remained.

The negroes giving too hot a reception, the whites kept a more respectful distance. Hovering now just out of reach of the hurtling hatchets, they, with a view to the close encounter which must soon come, sought to decoy the blacks into entirely disarming themselves of their most murderous weapons in a hand-to-hand fight, by foolishly flinging them, as missiles, short of the mark, into the sea. But ere long perceiving the stratagem, the negroes desisted, though not before many of them had to replace their lost hatchets with handspikes; an exchange which, as counted upon, proved in the end favorable to the assailants.

Meantime, with a strong wind, the ship still clove the water; the boats alternately falling behind, and pulling up, to discharge fresh volleys.

The fire was mostly directed towards the stern, since there, chiefly, the negroes, at present, were clustering. But to kill or maim the negroes was not the object. To take them, with the ship, was the object. To do it, the ship must be boarded; which could not be done by boats while she was sailing so fast.

A thought now struck the mate. Observing the Spanish boys still aloft, high as they could get, he called to them to descend to the yards, and cut adrift the sails. It was done. About this time, owing to causes hereafter to be shown, two Spaniards, in the dress of sailors and conspicuously showing themselves, were killed; not by volleys, but by deliberate marksman's shots; while, as it afterwards appeared, by one of the general discharges, Atufal, the black, and the Spaniard at the helm likewise were killed. What now, with the loss of the sails, and loss of leaders, the ship became unmanageable to the negroes.

With creaking masts, she came heavily round to the wind; the prow slowly swinging, into view of the boats, its skeleton gleaming in the horizontal moonlight, and casting a gigantic ribbed shadow upon the water. One extended arm of the ghost seemed beckoning the whites to avenge it.

"Follow your leader!" cried the mate; and, one on each bow, the boats boarded. Sealing-spears and cutlasses crossed hatchets and handspikes.

Huddled upon the long-boat amidships, the negresses raised a wailing chant, whose chorus was the clash of the steel.

For a time, the attack wavered; the negroes wedging themselves to beat it back; the half-repelled sailors, as yet unable to gain a footing, fighting as troopers in the saddle, one leg sideways flung over the bulwarks, and one without, plying their cutlasses like carters' whips. But in vain. They were almost overborne, when, rallying themselves into a squad as one man, with a huzza, they sprang inboard; where, entangled, they involuntarily separated again. For a few breaths' space, there was a vague, muffled, inner sound, as of submerged sword-fish rushing hither and thither through shoals of black-fish. Soon, in a reunited band, and joined by the Spanish seamen, the whites came to the surface, irresistibly driving the negroes toward the stern. But a barricade of casks and sacks, from side to side, had been thrown up by the mainmast. Here the negroes faced about, and though scorning peace or truce, yet fain would have had a respite. But, without pause, overleaping the barrier, the unflagging sailors again closed. Exhausted, the blacks now fought in despair. Their red tongues lolled, wolf-like, from their black mouths. But the pale sailors' teeth were set; not a word was spoken; and, in five minutes more, the ship was won.

Nearly a score of the negroes were killed. Exclusive of those by the balls, many were mangled; their wounds — mostly inflicted by the long-edged sealing-spears — resembling those shaven ones of the English at Preston Pans,[26] made by the poled scythes of the Highlanders. On the other side, none were killed, though several were wounded; some severely, including the mate. The surviving negroes were temporarily secured, and the ship, towed back into the harbor at midnight, once more lay anchored.

Omitting the incidents and arrangements ensuing, suffice it that, after two days spent in refitting, the two ships sailed in company for Conception, in Chili, and thence for Lima, in Peru; where, before the vice-regal courts, the whole affair, from the beginning, underwent investigation.

Though, midway on the passage, the ill-fated Spaniard, relaxed from constraint, showed some signs of regaining health with free-will; yet, agreeably to his own foreboding, shortly before arriving at Lima, he relapsed, finally becoming so reduced as to be carried ashore in arms. Hearing of his story and plight, one of the many religious institutions of the City of Kings opened an hospitable refuge to him, where both physician and priest were

---

26. *Preston Pans:* Battle in 1745 where a force of Scottish Highlanders led by Charles Edward Stuart (Bonnie Prince Charlie) routed the English army outside Edinburgh.

his nurses, and a member of the order volunteered to be his one special guardian and consoler, by night and by day.

The following extracts, translated from one of the official Spanish documents, will it is hoped, shed light on the preceding narrative, as well as, in the first place, reveal the true port of departure and true history of the San Dominick's voyage, down to the time of her touching at the island of St. Maria.

But, ere the extracts come, it may be well to preface them with a remark.

The document selected, from among many others, for partial translation, contains the deposition of Benito Cereno; the first taken in the case. Some disclosures therein were, at the time, held dubious for both learned and natural reasons. The tribunal inclined to the opinion that the deponent, not undisturbed in his mind by recent events, raved of some things which could never have happened. But subsequent depositions of the surviving sailors, bearing out the revelations of their captain in several of the strangest particulars, gave credence to the rest. So that the tribunal, in its final decision, rested its capital sentences upon statements which, had they lacked confirmation, it would have deemed it but duty to reject.

I, DON JOSE DE ABOS AND PADILLA, His Majesty's Notary for the Royal Revenue, and Register of this Province, and Notary Public of the Holy Crusade of this Bishopric, etc.

Do certify and declare, as much as is requisite in law, that, in the criminal cause commenced the twenty-fourth of the month of September, in the year seventeen hundred and ninety-nine, against the negroes of the ship San Dominick, the following declaration before me was made.

Declaration of the first witness, DON BENITO CERENO.

The same day, and month, and year, His Honor, Doctor Juan Martinez de Rozas, Councilor of the Royal Audience of this Kingdom, and learned in the law of this Intendency, ordered the captain of the ship San Dominick, Don Benito Cereno, to appear; which he did in his litter, attended by the monk Infelez; of whom he received the oath, which he took by God, our Lord, and a sign of the Cross; under which he promised to tell the truth of whatever he should know and should be asked; – and being interrogated agreeably to the tenor of the act commencing the process, he said, that on the twentieth of May last, he set sail with his ship from the port of Valparaiso, bound to that of

Callao; loaded with the produce of the country beside thirty
cases of hardware and one hundred and sixty blacks, of both
sexes, mostly belonging to Don Alexandro Aranda, gentleman, of
the city of Mendoza; that the crew of the ship consisted of thirty-
six men, beside the persons who went as passengers; that the
negroes were in part as follows:

*[Here, in the original, follows a list of some fifty names,
descriptions, and ages, compiled from certain recovered
documents of Aranda's, and also from recollections of the
deponent, from which portions only are extracted.]*

– One, from about eighteen to nineteen years, named José,
and this was the man that waited upon his master, Don Alexandro,
and who speaks well the Spanish, having served him four or five
years; * * * a mulatto, named Francesco, the cabin steward, of a
good person and voice, having sung in the Valparaiso churches,
native of the province of Buenos Ayres, aged about thirty-five
years * * * A smart negro, named Dago, who had been for many
years a grave-digger among the Spaniards, aged forty-six years.
* * * Four old negroes, born in Africa, from sixty to seventy, but
sound, calkers by trade, whose names are as follows: – the first
was named Mure, and he was killed (as was also his son named
Diamelo); the second, Natu; the third, Yola, likewise killed; the
fourth, Ghofan; and six full-grown negroes, aged from thirty to
forty-five, all raw, and born among the Ashantees – Matiluqui,
Yau, Lecbe, Mapenda, Yambaio, Akim; four of whom were killed;
* * * a powerful negro named Atufal, who, being supposed to
have been a chief in Africa, his owners set great store by him. * * *
And a small negro of Senegal, but some years among the
Spaniards, aged about thirty, which negro's name was Babo; * * *
that he does not remember the names of the others, but that still
expecting the residue of Don Alexandro's papers will be found, will
then take due account of them all, and remit to the court; * * *
and thirty-nine women and children of all ages.

[The catalogue over, the deposition goes on:]

* * * That all the negroes slept upon deck, as is customary in
this navigation, and none wore fetters, because the owner, his

friend Aranda, told him that they were all tractable; * * * that on
the seventh day after leaving port, at three o'clock in the morning,
all the Spaniards being asleep except the two officers on the watch,
who were the boatswain, Juan Robles, and the carpenter, Juan
Bautista Gayete, and the helmsman and his boy, the negroes
revolted suddenly, wounded dangerously the boatswain and the
carpenter, and successively killed eighteen men of those who
were sleeping upon deck, some with hand-spikes and hatchets,
and others by throwing them alive overboard, after tying them;
that of the Spaniards upon deck, they left about seven, as he
thinks, alive and tied, to manœuvre the ship, and three or four
more, who hid themselves, remained also alive. Although in the
act of revolt the negroes made themselves masters of the hatchway,
six or seven wounded went through it to the cockpit, without any
hindrance on their part; that during the act of revolt, the mate
and another person, whose name he does not recollect, attempted
to come up through the hatchway, but being quickly wounded,
they were obliged to return to the cabin; that the deponent resolved
at break of day to come up the companion-way, where the negro
Babo was, being the ringleader, and Atufal, who assisted him, and
having spoken to them, exhorted them to cease committing such
atrocities, asking them, at the same time, what they wanted and
intended to do, offering, himself, to obey their commands; that,
notwithstanding this, they threw, in his presence, three men, alive
and tied, overboard; that they told the deponent to come up, and
that they would not kill him; which having done, the negro Babo
asked him whether there were in those seas any negro countries
where they might be carried, and he answered them, No; that the
negro Babo afterwards told him to carry them to Senegal, or to
the neighboring islands of St. Nicolas; and he answered, that this
was impossible, on account of the great distance, the necessity
involved of rounding Cape Horn, the bad condition of the vessel,
the want of provisions, sails, and water; but that the negro Babo
replied to him he must carry them in any way; that they would do
and conform themselves to everything the deponent should require
as to eating and drinking; that after a long conference, being
absolutely compelled to please them, for they threatened him to
kill all the whites if they were not, at all events, carried to Senegal,
he told them that what was most wanting for the voyage was
water; that they would go near the coast to take it, and thence

they would proceed on their course; that the negro Babo agreed to it; and the deponent steered towards the intermediate ports, hoping to meet some Spanish or foreign vessel that would save them; that within ten or eleven days they saw the land, and continued their course by it in the vicinity of Nasca; that the deponent observed that the negroes were now restless and mutinous, because he did not effect the taking in of water, the negro Babo having required, with threats, that it should be done, without fail, the following day; he told him they saw plainly that the coast was steep, and the rivers designated in the maps were not to be found, with other reasons suitable to the circumstances; that the best way would be to go to the island of Santa Maria, where they might water and victual easily, it being a solitary island, as the foreigners did; that the deponent did not go to Pisco, that was near, nor make any other port of the coast, because the negro Babo had intimated to him several times, that he would kill all the whites the very moment he should perceive any city, town, or settlement of any kind on the shores to which they should be carried: that having determined to go to the island of Santa Maria, as the deponent had planned, for the purpose of trying whether, on the passage or near the island itself, they could find any vessel that should favor them, or whether he could escape from it in a boat to the neighboring coast of Arauco; to adopt the necessary means he immediately changed his course, steering for the island; that the negroes Babo and Atufal held daily conferences, in which they discussed what was necessary for their design of returning to Senegal, whether they were to kill all the Spaniards, and particularly the deponent; that eight days after parting from the coast of Nasca, the deponent being on the watch a little after day-break, and soon after the negroes had their meeting, the negro Babo came to the place where the deponent was, and told him that he had determined to kill his master, Don Alexandro Aranda, both because he and his companions could not otherwise be sure of their liberty, and that, to keep the seamen in subjection, he wanted to prepare a warning of what road they should be made to take did they or any of them oppose him; and that, by means of the death of Don Alexandro, that warning would best be given; but, that what this last meant, the deponent did not at the time comprehend, nor could not, further than that the death of Don Alexandro was intended; and moreover, the negro Babo proposed to the deponent to call the mate Raneds, who was sleeping in the cabin, before the thing was done, for fear, as the deponent understood it, that the mate, who was a good navigator, should be killed with Don Alexandro and the rest; that the deponent, who was the friend, from youth, of Don Alexandro, prayed and conjured, but all was useless; for the negro Babo answered him that the thing could not be prevented, and that all the Spaniards risked their death if they should attempt to frustrate his will in this matter, or any other; that, in this conflict, the deponent called the mate, Raneds, who was forced to go apart, and immediately the negro Babo commanded the Ashantee Matiluqui and the Ashantee Lecbe to go and commit the murder; that those two went down with hatchets to the berth of Don Alexandro; that, yet half alive and mangled, they dragged him on deck; that they were going to throw him overboard in that state, but the negro Babo stopped them, bidding the murder be completed on the deck before him, which was done, when, by his orders, the body was carried below, forward; that nothing more was seen of it by the deponent for three days; * * * that Don Alonzo Sidonia, an old man, long resident at Valparaiso, and lately appointed to a civil office in Peru, whither he had taken passage, was at the time sleeping in the berth opposite Don Alexandro's; that, awakening at his cries, surprised by them, and at the sight of the negroes with their bloody hatchets in their hands, he threw himself into the sea through a window which was near him, and was drowned, without it being in the power of the deponent to assist or take him up; * * * that, a short time after killing Aranda, they brought upon deck his german-cousin, of middle-age, Don Francisco Masa, of Mendoza, and the young Don Joaquin, Marques de Arambaolaza, then lately from Spain, with his Spanish servant Ponce, and the three young clerks of Aranda, José Morairi, Lorenzo Bargas, and Hermenegildo Gandix, all of Cadiz; that Don Joaquin and Hermenegildo Gandix, the negro Babo for purposes hereafter to appear, preserved alive; but Don Francisco Masa, José Morairi, and Lorenzo Bargas, with Ponce the servant, beside the boatswain, Juan Robles, the boatswain's mates, Manuel Viscaya and Roderigo Hurta, and four of the sailors, the negro Babo ordered to be thrown alive into the sea, although they made no resistance, nor begged for anything else but mercy; that the boatswain, Juan Robles, who knew how to swim, kept the longest above water, making acts of contrition, and, in the last words he uttered, charged this deponent to cause mass

to be said for his soul to our Lady of Succor; * * * that, during the
three days which followed, the deponent, uncertain what fate had
befallen the remains of Don Alexandro, frequently asked the negro
Babo where they were, and, if still on board, whether they were to
be preserved for interment ashore, entreating him so to order it;
that the negro Babo answered nothing till the fourth day, when at
sunrise, the deponent coming on deck, the negro Babo showed him
a skeleton, which had been substituted for the ship's proper figure-
head, the image of Christopher Colon, the discoverer of the New
World; that the negro Babo asked him whose skeleton that was,
and whether, from its whiteness, he should not think it a white's;
that, upon his covering his face, the negro Babo, coming close, said
words to this effect: "Keep faith with the blacks from here to
Senegal, or you shall in spirit, as now in body, follow your leader,"
pointing to the prow; * * * that the same morning the negro Babo
took by succession each Spaniard forward, and asked him whose
skeleton that was, and whether, from its whiteness, he should not
think it a white's; that each Spaniard covered his face; that then to
each the negro Babo repeated the words in the first place said to
the deponent; * * * that they (the Spaniards), being then assembled
aft, the negro Babo harangued them, saying that he had now done
all; that the deponent (as navigator for the negroes) might pursue
his course, warning him and all of them that they should, soul and
body, go the way of Don Alexandro if he saw them (the Spaniards)
speak or plot anything against them (the negroes) — a threat which
was repeated every day; that, before the events last mentioned, they
had tied the cook to throw him overboard, for it is not known what
thing they heard him speak, but finally the negro Babo spared his
life, at the request of the deponent; that a few days after, the
deponent, endeavoring not to omit any means to preserve the lives
of the remaining whites, spoke to the negroes peace and
tranquillity, and agreed to draw up a paper, signed by the deponent
and the sailors who could write, as also by the negro Babo, for
himself and all the blacks, in which the deponent obliged himself
to carry them to Senegal, and they not to kill any more, and he
formally to make over to them the ship, with the cargo, with which
they were for that time satisfied and quieted. * * * But the next day,
the more surely to guard against the sailors' escape, the negro Babo
commanded all the boats to be destroyed but the long-boat, which
was unseaworthy, and another, a cutter in good condition, which,

knowing it would yet be wanted for towing the water casks, he had
it lowered down into the hold.

* * * * *

*[Various particulars of the prolonged and perplexed
navigation ensuing here follow, with incidents of a calamitous
calm, from which portion one passage is extracted, to wit:]*

– That on the fifth day of the calm, all on board suffering much
from the heat, and want of water, and five having died in fits,
and mad, the negroes became irritable, and for a chance gesture,
which they deemed suspicious – though it was harmless – made
by the mate, Raneds, to the deponent, in the act of handing a
quadrant, they killed him; but that for this they afterwards were
sorry, the mate being the only remaining navigator on board,
except the deponent.

* * * * *

– That omitting other events, which daily happened, and which
can only serve uselessly to recall past misfortunes and conflicts,
after seventy-three days' navigation, reckoned from the time they
sailed from Nasca, during which they navigated under a scanty
allowance of water, and were afflicted with the calms before
mentioned, they at last arrived at the island of Santa Maria, on the
seventeenth of the month of August, at about six o'clock in the
afternoon, at which hour they cast anchor very near the American
ship, Bachelor's Delight, which lay in the same bay, commanded by
the generous Captain Amasa Delano; but at six o'clock in the
morning, they had already descried the port, and the negroes
became uneasy, as soon as at distance they saw the ship, not
having expected to see one there; that the negro Babo pacified
them, assuring them that no fear need be had; that straightway he
ordered the figure on the bow to be covered with canvas, as for
repairs, and had the decks a little set in order; that for a time the
negro Babo and the negro Atufal conferred; that the negro Atufal
was for sailing away, but the negro Babo would not, and, by
himself, cast about what to do; that at last he came to the
deponent, proposing to him to say and do all that the deponent
declares to have said and done to the American captain;
* * * * * * that the negro Babo warned him that if he varied in the

least, or uttered any word, or gave any look that should give the least intimation of the past events or present state, he would instantly kill him, with all his companions, showing a dagger, which he carried hid, saying something which, as he understood it, meant that the dagger would be alert as his eye; that the negro Babo then announced the plan to all his companions, which pleased them; that he then, the better to disguise the truth, devised many expedients, in some of them uniting deceit and defense; that of this sort was the device of the six Ashantees before named, who were his bravoes; that them he stationed on the break of the poop, as if to clean certain hatchets (in cases, which were part of the cargo), but in reality to use them, and distribute them at need, and at a given word he told them; that, among other devices, was the device of presenting Atufal, his right-hand man, as chained, though in a moment the chains could be dropped; that in every particular he informed the deponent what part he was expected to enact in every device, and what story he was to tell on every occasion, always threatening him with instant death if he varied in the least: that, conscious that many of the negroes would be turbulent, the negro Babo appointed the four aged negroes, who were calkers, to keep what domestic order they could on the decks; that again and again he harangued the Spaniards and his companions; informing them of his intent, and of his devices, and of the invented story that this deponent was to tell, charging them lest any of them varied from that story; that these arrangements were made and matured during the interval of two or three hours, between their first sighting the ship and the arrival on board of Captain Amasa Delano; that this happened about half-past seven o'clock in the morning, Captain Amasa Delano coming in his boat, and all gladly receiving him; that the deponent, as well as he could force himself, acting then the part of principal owner, and a free captain of the ship, told Captain Amasa Delano, when called upon, that he came from Buenos Ayres, bound to Lima, with three hundred negroes; that off Cape Horn, and in a subsequent fever, many negroes had died; that also, by similar casualties, all the sea officers and the greatest part of the crew had died.

* * * * *

[And so the deposition goes on, circumstantially recounting the fictitious story dictated to the deponent by Babo, and through

*the deponent imposed upon Captain Delano; and also recounting
the friendly offers of Captain Delano, with other things, but all of
which is here omitted. After the fictitious, strange story, etc., the
deposition proceeds:]*

— that the generous Captain Amasa Delano remained on board
all the day, till he left the ship anchored at six o'clock in the
evening, deponent speaking to him always of his pretended
misfortunes, under the forementioned principles, without
having had it in his power to tell a single word, or give him the
least hint, that he might know the truth and state of things;
because the negro Babo, performing the office of an officious
servant with all the appearance of submission of the humble
slave, did not leave the deponent one moment; that this was in
order to observe the deponent's actions and words, for the negro
Babo understands well the Spanish; and besides, there were
thereabout some others who were constantly on the watch, and
likewise understood the Spanish; * * * that upon one occasion,
while deponent was standing on the deck conversing with
Amasa Delano, by a secret sign the negro Babo drew him (the
deponent) aside, the act appearing as if originating with the
deponent; that then, he being drawn aside, the negro Babo
proposed to him to gain from Amasa Delano full particulars
about his ship, and crew, and arms; that the deponent asked "For
what?" that the negro Babo answered he might conceive; that,
grieved at the prospect of what might overtake the generous
Captain Amasa Delano, the deponent at first refused to ask the
desired questions, and used every argument to induce the negro
Babo to give up this new design; that the negro Babo showed
the point of his dagger; that, after the information had been
obtained, the negro Babo again drew him aside, telling him that
that very night he (the deponent) would be captain of two ships,
instead of one, for that, great part of the American's ship's crew
being to be absent fishing, the six Ashantees, without any one
else, would easily take it; that at this time he said other things to
the same purpose; that no entreaties availed; that, before Amasa
Delano's coming on board, no hint had been given touching the
capture of the American ship: that to prevent this project the
deponent was powerless; * * * — that in some things his memory
is confused he cannot distinctly recall every event; * * * — that

as soon as they had cast anchor at six of the clock in the
evening, as has before been stated, the American Captain took
leave to return to his vessel; that upon a sudden impulse, which
the deponent believes to have come from God and his angels, he,
after the farewell had been said, followed the generous Captain
Amasa Delano as far as the gunwale, where he stayed, under
pretense of taking leave, until Amasa Delano should have been
seated in his boat; that on shoving off, the deponent sprang from
the gunwale into the boat, and fell into it, he knows not how, God
guarding him; that –

* * * * *

*[Here, in the original, follows the account of what further
happened at the escape, and how the San Dominick was
retaken, and of the passage to the coast; including in the recital
many expressions of "eternal gratitude" to the "generous Captain
Amasa Delano." The deposition then proceeds with recapitulatory
remarks, and a partial renumeration of the negroes, making
record of their individual part in the past events, with a view to
furnishing, according to command of the court, the data whereon
to found the criminal sentences to be pronounced. From this
portion is the following:]*

– That he believes that all the negroes, though not in
the first place knowing to the design of revolt, when it was
accomplished, approved it. * * * That the negro, José, eighteen
years old, and in the personal service of Don Alexandro, was the
one who communicated the information to the negro Babo,
about the state of things in the cabin, before the revolt; that this
is known, because, in the preceding midnights, he used to come
from his berth, which was under his master's, in the cabin, to the
deck where the ringleader and his associates were, and had
secret conversations with the negro Babo, in which he was
several times seen by the mate; that, one night, the mate drove
him away twice; * * that this same negro José, was the one who,
without being commanded to do so by the negro Babo, as Lecbe
and Matiluqui were, stabbed his master, Don Alexandro, after he
had been dragged half-lifeless to the deck; * * that the mulatto
steward, Francesco, was of the first band of revolters, that he
was, in all things, the creature and tool of the negro Babo; that,
to make his court, he, just before a repast in the cabin, proposed,

to the negro Babo, poisoning a dish for the generous Captain
Amasa Delano; this is known and believed, because the negroes
have said it; but that the negro Babo, having another design,
forbade Francesco; * * that the Ashantee Lecbe was one of the
worst of them; for that, on the day the ship was retaken, he
assisted in the defense of her, with a hatchet in each hand, with
one of which he wounded, in the breast, the chief mate of Amasa
Delano, in the first act of boarding; this all knew; that, in sight
of the deponent, Lecbe struck, with a hatchet, Don Francisco
Masa when, by the negro Babo's orders, he was carrying him to
throw him overboard, alive; beside participating in the murder,
before mentioned, of Don Alexandro Aranda, and others of the
cabin-passengers; that, owing to the fury with which the
Ashantees fought in the engagement with the boats, but this
Lecbe and Yau survived; that Yau was bad as Lecbe; that Yau was
the man who, by Babo's command, willingly prepared the
skeleton of Don Alexandro, in a way the negroes afterwards told
the deponent, but which he, so long as reason is left him, can
never divulge; that Yau and Lecbe were the two who, in a calm by
night, riveted the skeleton to the bow; this also the negroes told
him; that the negro Babo was he who traced the inscription
below it; that the negro Babo was the plotter from first to last; he
ordered every murder, and was the helm and keel of the revolt;
that Atufal was his lieutenant in all; but Atufal, with his own
hand, committed no murder; nor did the negro Babo; * * that
Atufal was shot, being killed in the fight with the boats, ere
boarding; * * that the negresses, of age, were knowing to the
revolt, and testified themselves satisfied at the death of their
master, Don Alexandro; that, had the negroes not restrained
them, they would have tortured to death, instead of simply
killing, the Spaniards slain by command of the negro Babo; that
the negresses used their utmost influence to have the deponent
made away with; that, in the various acts of murder, they sang
songs and danced – not gaily, but solemnly; and before the
engagement with the boats, as well as during the action, they
sang melancholy songs to the negroes, and that this melancholy
tone was more inflaming than a different one would have been,
and was so intended; that all this is believed, because the
negroes have said it.

— that of the thirty-six men of the crew exclusive of the passengers,
(all of whom are now dead), which the deponent had knowledge
of, six only remained alive, with four cabin-boys and ship-boys,
not included with the crew; * * — that the negroes broke an arm
of one of the cabin-boys and gave him strokes with hatchets.

*[Then follow various random disclosures referring to various
periods of time. The following are extracted:]*

— That during the presence of Captain Amasa Delano on board,
some attempts were made by the sailors, and one by Hermenegildo
Gandix, to convey hints to him of the true state of affairs; but
that these attempts were ineffectual, owing to fear of incurring
death, and furthermore owing to the devices which offered
contradictions to the true state of affairs; as well as owing to the
generosity and piety of Amasa Delano incapable of sounding
such wickedness; * * * that Luys Galgo, a sailor about sixty
years of age, and formerly of the king's navy, was one of those
who sought to convey tokens to Captain Amasa Delano; but his
intent, though undiscovered, being suspected, he was, on a
pretense, made to retire out of sight, and at last into the hold,
and there was made away with. This the negroes have since said;
* * * that one of the ship-boys feeling, from Captain Amasa
Delano's presence, some hopes of release, and not having
enough prudence, dropped some chance-word respecting his
expectations, which being overheard and understood by a slave-
boy with whom he was eating at the time, the latter struck him
on the head with a knife, inflicting a bad wound, but of which
the boy is now healing; that likewise, not long before the ship
was brought to anchor, one of the seamen, steering at the time,
endangered himself by letting the blacks remark some expression
in his countenance, arising from a cause similar to the above;
but this sailor, by his heedful after conduct, escaped; * * * that
these statements are made to show the court that from the
beginning to the end of the revolt, it was impossible for the
deponent and his men to act otherwise than they did; * * * — that
the third clerk, Hermenegildo Gandix, who before had been forced
to live among the seamen, wearing a seaman's habit, and in all
respects appearing to be one for the time; he, Gandix, was killed

by a musket-ball fired through a mistake from the American boats
before boarding; having in his fright ran up the mizzen-rigging,
calling to the boats – "don't board," lest upon their boarding the
negroes should kill him; that this inducing the Americans to
believe he some way favored the cause of the negroes, they fired
two balls at him, so that he fell wounded from the rigging, and
was drowned in the sea; * * * – that the young Don Joaquin,
Marques de Arambaolaza, like Hermenegildo Gandix, the third
clerk, was degraded to the office and appearance of a common
seaman; that upon one occasion when Don Joaquin shrank, the
negro Babo commanded the Ashantee Lecbe to take tar and heat
it, and pour it upon Don Joaquin's hands; * * * – that Don Joaquin
was killed owing to another mistake of the Americans, but one
impossible to be avoided, as upon the approach of the boats, Don
Joaquin, with a hatchet tied edge out and upright to his hand,
was made by the negroes to appear on the bulwarks; whereupon,
seen with arms in his hands and in a questionable attitude, he
was shot for a renegade seaman; * * * – that on the person of
Don Joaquin was found secreted a jewel, which, by papers that
were discovered, proved to have been meant for the shrine of our
Lady of Mercy in Lima; a votive offering, beforehand prepared
and guarded, to attest his gratitude, when he should have landed
in Peru, his last destination, for the safe conclusion of his entire
voyage from Spain; * * * – that the jewel, with the other effects
of the late Don Joaquin, is in the custody of the brethren of the
Hospital de Sacerdotes, awaiting the disposition of the honorable
court; * * * – that, owing to the condition of the deponent, as
well as the haste in which the boats departed for the attack, the
Americans were not forewarned that there were, among the
apparent crew, a passenger and one of the clerks disguised by
the negro Babo; * * * – that, beside the negroes killed in the
action, some were killed after the capture and re-anchoring at
night, when shackled to the ring-bolts on deck; that these deaths
were committed by the sailors, ere they could be prevented. That
so soon as informed of it, Captain Amasa Delano used all his
authority, and, in particular with his own hand, struck down
Martinez Gola, who, having found a razor in the pocket of an old
jacket of his, which one of the shackled negroes had on, was
aiming it at the negro's throat; that the noble Captain Amasa
Delano also wrenched from the hand of Bartholomew Barlo, a

dagger secreted at the time of the massacre of the whites, with which he was in the act of stabbing a shackled negro, who, the same day, with another negro, had thrown him down and jumped upon him; * * * – that, for all the events, befalling through so long a time, during which the ship was in the hands of the negro Babo, he cannot here give account; but that, what he has said is the most substantial of what occurs to him at present, and is the truth under the oath which he has taken; which declaration he affirmed and ratified, after hearing it read to him.

He said that he is twenty-nine years of age, and broken in body and mind; that when finally dismissed by the court, he shall not return home to Chili, but betake himself to the monastery on Mount Agonia without; and signed with his honor, and crossed himself, and, for the time, departed as he came, in his litter, with the monk Infelez, to the Hospital de Sacerdotes.

BENITO CERENO.

DOCTOR ROZAS.

If the Deposition have served as the key to fit into the lock of the complications which precede it, then, as a vault whose door has been flung back, the San Dominick's hull lies open to-day.

Hitherto the nature of this narrative, besides rendering the intricacies in the beginning unavoidable, has more or less required that many things, instead of being set down in the order of occurrence, should be retrospectively, or irregularly given; this last is the case with the following passages, which will conclude the account:

During the long, mild voyage to Lima, there was, as before hinted, a period during which the sufferer a little recovered his health, or, at least in some degree, his tranquillity. Ere the decided relapse which came, the two captains had many cordial conversations – their fraternal unreserve in singular contrast with former withdrawments.

Again and again, it was repeated, how hard it had been to enact the part forced on the Spaniard by Babo.

"Ah, my dear friend," Don Benito once said, "at those very times when you thought me so morose and ungrateful, nay, when, as you now admit, you half thought me plotting your murder, at those very times my heart was frozen; I could not look at you, thinking of what, both on board this ship and your own, hung, from other hands, over my kind benefactor. And as God lives, Don Amasa, I know not whether desire for my own safety alone could have nerved me to that leap into your boat, had it not been for the thought that, did you, unenlightened, return to your ship, you, my best friend, with all who might be with you, stolen upon, that night, in your hammocks, would never in this world have wakened again. Do but think how you walked this deck, how you sat in this cabin, every inch of ground mined into honey-combs under you. Had I dropped the least hint, made the least advance towards an understanding between us, death, explosive death – yours as mine – would have ended the scene."

"True, true," cried Captain Delano, starting, "you have saved my life, Don Benito, more than I yours; saved it, too, against my knowledge and will."

"Nay, my friend," rejoined the Spaniard, courteous even to the point of religion, "God charmed your life, but you saved mine. To think of some things you did – those smilings and chattings, rash pointings and gestur-ings. For less than these, they slew my mate, Raneds; but you had the Prince of Heaven's safe conduct through all ambuscades."

"Yes, all is owing to Providence, I know; but the temper of my mind that morning was more than commonly pleasant, while the sight of so much suffering, more apparent than real, added to my good nature, compassion, and charity, happily interweaving the three. Had it been otherwise, doubt-less, as you hint, some of my interferences might have ended unhappily enough. Besides that, those feelings I spoke of enabled me to get the bet-ter of momentary distrust, at times when acuteness might have cost me my life, without saving another's. Only at the end did my suspicions get the better of me, and you know how wide of the mark they then proved."

"Wide, indeed," said Don Benito, sadly; "you were with me all day; stood with me, sat with me, talked with me, looked at me, ate with me, drank with me; and yet, your last act was to clutch for a monster, not only an innocent man, but the most pitiable of all men. To such degree may malign machi-nations and deceptions impose. So far may even the best man err, in judging the conduct of one with the recesses of whose condition he is not acquainted. But you were forced to it; and you were in time undeceived. Would that, in both respects, it was so ever, and with all men."

"You generalize, Don Benito; and mournfully enough. But the past is passed; why moralize upon it? Forget it. See, yon bright sun has forgotten it all, and the blue sea, and the blue sky; these have turned over new leaves."

"Because they have no memory," he dejectedly replied; "because they are not human."

"But these mild trades that now fan your cheek, do they not come with a human-like healing to you? Warm friends, steadfast friends are the trades."

"With their steadfastness they but waft me to my tomb, señor," was the foreboding response.

"You are saved," cried Captain Delano, more and more astonished and pained; "you are saved; what has cast such a shadow upon you?"

"The negro."

There was silence, while the moody man sat, slowly and unconsciously gathering his mantle about him, as if it were a pall.

There was no more conversation that day.

But if the Spaniard's melancholy sometimes ended in muteness upon topics like the above, there were others upon which he never spoke at all; on which, indeed, all his old reserves were piled. Pass over the worst, and, only to elucidate, let an item or two of these be cited. The dress so precise and costly, worn by him on the day whose events have been narrated, had not willingly been put on. And that silver-mounted sword, apparent symbol of despotic command, was not, indeed, a sword, but the ghost of one. The scabbard, artificially stiffened, was empty.

As for the black – whose brain, not body, had schemed and led the revolt, with the plot – his slight frame, inadequate to that which it held, had at once yielded to the superior muscular strength of his captor, in the boat. Seeing all was over, he uttered no sound, and could not be forced to. His aspect seemed to say, since I cannot do deeds, I will not speak words. Put in irons in the hold, with the rest, he was carried to Lima.[27] During the passage Don Benito did not visit him. Nor then, nor at any time after, would he look at him. Before the tribunal he refused. When pressed by the judges he fainted. On the testimony of the sailors alone rested the legal identity of Babo.

Some months after, dragged to the gibbet at the tail of a mule, the black met his voiceless end. The body was burned to ashes; but for many days, the head, that hive of subtlety, fixed on a pole in the Plaza, met, unabashed, the gaze of the whites; and across the Plaza looked towards St. Bartholomew's church, in whose vaults slept then, as now, the recovered bones of Aranda; and across the Rimac bridge looked towards the monastery, on Mount Agonia without; where, three months after being dismissed by the court, Benito Cereno, borne on the bier, did, indeed, follow his leader.

27. *Lima:* In *Moby-Dick* (1851), Melville describes Lima in "The Whiteness of the Whale" as "the strangest, saddest city thou can'st see" and in "The Town-Ho's Story" as the epitome of the world's worst vices: "No need to travel! The world's one Lima" (193, 250). An article titled "Lima and the Limanians," which describes the Plaza in striking detail and gives a full history of European colonialism in Peru, appeared in the same issue of *Harper's New Monthly Magazine* in which "The Town-Ho's Story" was published separately from *Moby-Dick* (October 1851).

From A Narrative of Voyages and Travels, in the Northern and Southern Hemispheres: Comprising Three Voyages Round the World, Together with a Voyage of Survey and Discovery in the Pacific Ocean and Oriental Islands

Amasa Delano

Chapter XVIII

IN INTRODUCING THE ACCOUNT of the capture of the Spanish ship Tryal, I shall first give an extract from the journal of the ship Perseverance, taken on board that ship at the time, by the officer who had the care of the log book.

"Wednesday, February 20th, commenced with light airs from the north east, and thick foggy weather. At six a.m. observed a sail opening round the south head of St. Maria, coming into the bay. It proved to be a ship. The captain took the whale boat and crew, and went on board her. As the wind was very light, so that a vessel would not have much more than steerage way at the time; observed that the ship acted very awkwardly. At ten a.m. the boat returned. Mr. Luther informed that Captain Delano had remained on board her, and that she was a

Spaniard from Buenos Ayres, four months and twenty six days out of port, with slaves on board; and that the ship was in great want of water, had buried many white men and slaves on her passage, and that Captain Delano had sent for a large boat load of water, some fresh fish, sugar, bread, pumpkins, and bottled cider, all of which articles were immediately sent. At twelve o'clock (Meridian) calm. At two p.m. the large boat returned from the Spaniards, had left our water casks on board her. At four p.m. a breeze sprung up from the southern quarter, which brought the Spanish ship into the roads. She anchored about two cables length to the south east of our ship. Immediately after she anchored, our captain with his boat was shoving off from along side the Spanish ship; when to his great surprise the Spanish captain leaped into the boat, and called out in Spanish, that the slaves on board had risen and murdered many of the people; and that he did not then command her; on which manœuvre, several of the Spaniards who remained on board jumped overboard, and swam for our boat, and were picked up by our people. The Spaniards, who remained on board, hurried up the rigging, as high aloft as they could possibly get, and called out repeatedly for help – that they should be murdered by the slaves. Our captain came immediately on board, and brought the Spanish captain and the men who were picked up in the water; but before the boat arrived, we observed that the slaves had cut the Spanish ship adrift. On learning this, our captain hailed, and ordered the ports to be got up, and the guns cleared; but unfortunately, we could not bring but one of our guns to bear on the ship. We fired five or six shot with it, but could not bring her too [to]. We soon observed her making sail, and standing directly out of the bay. We dispatched two boats well manned, and well armed after her, who, after much trouble, boarded the ship and retook her. But unfortunately in the business, Mr. Rufus Low, our chief officer, who commanded the party, was desperately wounded in the breast, by being stabbed with a pike, by one of the slaves. We likewise had one man badly wounded and two or three slightly. To continue the misfortune, the chief office[r] of the Spanish ship, who was compelled by the slaves to steer her out of the bay, received two very bad wounds, one in the side, and one through the thigh, both from musket balls. One Spaniard, a gentleman passenger on board, was likewise killed by a musket ball. We have not rightly ascertained what number of slaves were killed; but we believe seven, and a great number wounded. Our people brought the ship in, and came to nearly where she first anchored, at about two o'clock in the morning of the 21st. At six a.m. the two captains went on board the Spanish ship; took with them irons from our ship, and doubled [double] ironed all the remaining men of the slaves who were living. Left

Mr. Brown, our second officer, in charge of the ship, the gunner with him as mate, and eight other hands; together with the survivors of the Spanish crew. The captain, and chief officer, were removed to our ship, the latter for the benefit of having his wounds better attended to with us, than he could have had them on board his own ship. At nine a.m. the two captains returned, having put every thing aright, as they supposed, on board the Spanish ship.

"The Spanish captain then informed us that he was compelled by the slaves to say, that he was from Buenos Ayres, bound to Lima: that he was not from Buenos Ayres, but sailed on the 20th of December last from Valparaiso for Lima, with upwards of seventy slaves on board; that on the 26th of December, the slaves rose upon the ship, and took possession of her, and put to death eighteen white men, and threw overboard at different periods after, seven more; that the slaves had commanded him to go to Senegal; that he had kept to sea until his water was expended, and had made this port to get it; and also with a view to save his own and the remainder of his people's lives if possible, by run[n]ing away from his ship with his boat."

I shall here add some remarks of my own, to what is stated above from the ship's journal, with a view of giving the reader a correct understanding of the peculiar situation under which we were placed at the time this affair happened. We were in a worse situation to effect any important enterprize than I had been in during the voyage. We had been from home a year and a half, and had not made enough to amount to twenty dollars for each of my people, who were all on shares, and our future prospects were not very flattering. To make our situation worse, I had found after leaving New Holland, on mustering my people, that I had seventeen men, most of whom had been convicts at Botany bay. They had secreted themselves on board without my knowledge. This was a larger number than had been inveigled away from me at the same place, by people who had been convicts, and were then employed at places that we visited. The men whom we lost were all of them extraordinarily good men. This exchange materially altered the quality of the crew. Three of the Botany-bay-men were outlawed convicts; they had been shot at many times, and several times wounded. After making this bad exchange, my crew were refractory; the convicts were ever unfaithful, and took all the advantage that opportunity gave them. But sometimes exercising very strict discipline, and giving them good wholesome floggings; and at other times treating them with the best I had, or could get, according as their deeds deserved, I managed them without much difficulty during the passage across the South Pacific Ocean; and all the time I had been on the coast of Chili. I had lately been at the islands of St. Ambrose and St. Felix, and left there fifteen of my best men, with the view of procuring seals; and left that place in company with my consort the Pilgrim. We appointed Massa Fuero as our place of rendezvous, and if we did not meet there, again to rendezvous at St. Maria. I proceeded to the first place appointed; the Pilgrim had not arrived. I then determined to take a look at Juan Fernandez, and see if we could find any seals, as some persons had informed me they were to be found on some part of the island. I accordingly visited that place, as has been stated; from thence I proceeded to St. Maria; and arrived the 13th of February at that place, where we commonly find visitors. We found the ship Mars of Nantucket, commanded by Captain Jonathan Barney. The day we arrived, three of my Botany bay men run from the boat when on shore. The next day, (the 14th) I was informed by Captain Barney, that some of my convict men had planned to run away with one of my boats, and go over to the main. This information he obtained through the medium of his people. I examined into the affair, and was satisfied as to the truth of it; set five more of the above description of men on shore, making eight in all I had gotten clear of in two days. Captain Barney sailed about the 17th, and left me quite alone. I continued in that unpleasant situation till the 20th, never at any time after my arrival at this place, daring to let my whale boat be in the water fifteen minutes unless I was in her myself, from a fear that some of my people would run away with her. I always hoisted her in on deck the moment I came along side, by which means I had the advantage of them; for should they run away with any other boat belonging to the ship, I could overtake them with the whale boat, which they very well knew. They were also well satisfied of the reasons why that boat was always kept on board, except when in my immediate use. During this time, I had no fear from them, except of their running away. Under these disadvantages the Spanish ship Tryal made her appearance on the morning of the 20th, as has been stated; and I had in the course of the day the satisfaction of seeing the great utility of good discipline. In every part of the business of the Tryal, not one disaffected word was spoken by the men, but all flew to obey the commands they received; and to their credit it should be recorded, that no men ever behaved better than they, under such circumstances. When it is considered that we had but two boats, one a whale boat, and the other built by ourselves, while on the coast of New Holland, which was very little larger than the whale boat; both of them were clinker built, one of cedar, and the other not much stouter; with only twenty men to board and carry a ship, containing so many slaves, made desperate by their situation; for they were certain, if taken, to suffer death; and when arriving along side of the ship, they might have staved the bottom of the boats, by heaving into them a ballast stone or log of wood of twenty pounds: when all these things are taken into view, the reader may conceive of the hazardous nature of the enterprise, and the skill and the intrepidity which were requisite to carry it into execution.

On the afternoon of the 19th, before night, I sent the boatswain with the large boat and seine to try if he could catch some fish; he returned at night with but few, observing that the morning would be better, if he went early. I then wished him to go as early as he thought proper, and he accordingly went at four o'clock. At sunrise, or about that time, the officer who commanded the deck, came down to me while I was in my cot, with information that a sail was just opening round the south point, or head of the island. I immediately rose, went on deck, and observed that she was too near the land, on account of a reef that lay off the head; and at the same time remarked to my people, that she must be a stranger, and I did not well understand what she was about. Some of them observed that they did not know who she was, or what she was doing; but that they were accustomed to see vessels shew their colours, when coming into a port. I ordered the whale boat to be hoisted out and manned, which was accordingly done. Presuming the vessel was from sea, and had been many days out, without perhaps fresh provisions, we put the fish which had been caught the night before into the boat, to be presented if necessary. Every thing being soon ready, as I thought the strange ship was in danger, we made all the haste in our power to get on board, that we might prevent her getting on the reefs; but before we came near her, the wind headed her off, and she was doing well. I went along side, and saw the decks were filled with slaves. As soon as I got on deck, the captain, mate, people and slaves, crowded around me to relate their stories, and to make known their grievances; which could not but impress me with feelings of pity for their sufferings. They told me they had no water, as is related in their different accounts and depositions. After promising to relieve all the wants they had mentioned, I ordered the fish to be put on board, and sent the whale boat to our ship, with orders that the large boat, as soon as she returned from fishing, should take a set of gang casks to the watering place, fill them, and bring it for their relief as soon as possible. I also ordered the small boat to take what fish the large one had caught, and what soft bread they had baked, some pumpkins, some sugar, and bottled cider, and return to me without delay. The boat left me on board the Spanish ship, went to our own, and executed the orders; and returned to me again about eleven o'clock. At noon the large boat came with the water, which I was obliged to serve out to them myself, to keep them [from] drinking so much as to do themselves injury. I gave them at first one gill each, an hour after, half a pint, and the third hour, a pint. Afterward, I permit[t]ed them to drink as they pleased. They all looked up to me as a benefactor; and as I was deceived in them, I did them every possible kindness. Had it been otherwise there is no doubt I should have fallen a victim to their power. It was to my great advantage, that, on this occasion, the temperament of my mind was unusually pleasant. The apparent sufferings of those about me had softened my feelings into sympathy; or, doubtless my interference with some of their transactions would have cost me my life. The Spanish captain had evidently lost much of his authority over the slaves, whom he appeared to fear, and whom he was unwilling in any case to oppose. An instance of this occurred in the conduct of the four cabin boys, spoken of by the captain. They were eating with the slave boys on the main deck, when, (as I was afterwards informed) the Spanish boys, feeling some hopes of release, and not having prudence sufficient to keep silent, some words dropped respecting their expectations, which were understood by the slave boys. One of them gave a stroke with a knife on the head of one of the Spanish boys, which penetrated to the bone, in a cut four inches in length. I saw this and inquired what it meant. The captain replied, that it was merely the sport of the boys, who had fallen out. I told him it appeared to me to be rather serious sport, as the wound had caused the boy to lose about a quart of blood. Several similar instances of unruly conduct, which, agreeably to my manner of thinking, demanded immediate resistance and punishment, were thus easily winked at, and passed over. I felt willing however to make some allowance even for conduct so gross, when I considered them to have been broken down with fatigue and long suffering.

The act of the negro, who kept constantly at the elbows of Don Bonito and myself, I should, at any other time, have immediately resented; and although it excited my wonder, that his commander should allow this extraordinary liberty, I did not remonstrate against it, until it became troublesome to myself. I wished to have some private conversation with the captain alone, and the negro as usual following us into the cabin, I requested the captain to send him on deck, as the business about which we were to talk could not be conveniently communicated in presence of a third person. I spoke in Spanish, and the negro understood me. The captain assured me, that his remaining with us would be of no disservice; that he had made him his confidant and companion since he had lost so many of his officers and men. He had introduced him to me before, as captain of the slaves, and told me he kept them in good order. I was alone with them, or rather on board by myself, for three or four hours, during the absence of my boat, at which time the ship drifted out with the current three leagues from my own, when the breeze sprung up from the south east. It was nearly four o'clock in the afternoon. We ran the ship as near to the Perseverance as we could without either ship's swinging afoul the other. After the Spanish ship was anchored, I invited the captain to go on board my ship and take tea or coffee with me. His answer was short and seemingly reserved; and his air very different from that with which he had received my assistance. As I was at a loss to account for this change in his demeanour, and knew he had seen nothing in my conduct to justify it, and as I felt certain that he treated me with intentional neglect; in return I became less sociable, and said little to him. After I had ordered my boat to be hauled up and manned, and as I was going to the side of the vessel, in order to get into her, Don Bonito came to me, gave my hand a hearty squeeze, and, as I thought, seemed to feel the weight of the cool treatment with which I had retaliated. I had committed a mistake in attributing his apparent coldness to neglect; and as soon as the discovery was made, I was happy to rectify it, by a prompt renewal of friendly intercourse. He continued to hold my hand fast till I stepped off the gunwale down the side, when he let it go, and stood making me compliments. When I had seated myself in the boat, and ordered her to be shoved off, the people having their oars up on end, she fell off at a sufficient distance to leave room for the oars to drop. After they were down, the Spanish captain, to my great astonishment, leaped from the gunwale of the ship into the middle of our boat. As soon as he had recovered a little, he called out in so alarming a manner, that I could not understand him; and the Spanish sailors were then seen jumping overboard and making for our boat. These proceedings excited the wonder of us all. The officer whom I had with me anxiously inquired into their meaning. I smiled and told him, that I neither knew, nor cared; but it seemed the captain was trying to impress his people with a belief that we intended to run away with him. At this moment one of my Portuguese sailors in the boat, spoke to me, and gave me to understand what Don Bonito said. I desired the captain to come aft and sit down by my side, and in a calm deliberate manner relate the whole affair[.] In the mean time the boat was employed in picking up the men who had jumped from the ship. They had picked up three, (leaving one in the water till after the boat had put the Spanish captain and myself on board my ship,) when my officer observed the cable was cut, and the ship was swinging. I hailed the Perseverance, ordering the ports got up, and the guns run out as soon as possible. We pulled as fast as we could on board; and then despatched the boat for the man who was left in the water, whom we succeeded to save alive.

We soon had our guns ready; but the Spanish ship had dropped so far astern of the Perseverance, that we could bring but one gun to bear on her, which was the after one. This was fired six times, without any other effect than cutting away the fore top-mast stay, and some other small ropes which were no hindrance to her going away. She was soon out of reach of our shot, steering out of the bay. We then had some other calculations to make. Our ship was moored with two bower anchors, which were all the cables or anchors of that description we had. To slip and leave them would be to break our policy of insurance by a deviation, against which I would here caution the masters of all vessels. It should always be borne in mind, that to do any thing which will destroy the guaranty of their policies, how great soever may be the inducement, and how generous soever the motive, is not justifiable; for should any accident subsequently occur, whereby a loss might accrue to the underwriters, they will be found ready enough, and sometimes too ready, to avail themselves of the opportunity to be released from responsibility; and the damage must necessarily be sustained by the owners. This is perfectly right. The law has wisely restrained the powers of the insured, that the insurer should not be subject to imposition, or abuse. All bad consequences may be avoided by one who has a knowledge of his duty, and is disposed faithfully to obey its dictates.

At length, without much loss of time, I came to a determination to pursue, and take the ship with my two boats. On inquiring of the captain what fire arms they had on board the Tryal, he answered, they had none which they could use; that he had put the few they had out of order, so that they could make no defence with them; and furthermore, that they did not understand their use, if they were in order. He observed at the same time, that if I attempted to take her with boats we should all be killed; for the negros were such bravos and so desperate, that there would be no such thing as conquering them. I saw the man in the situation that I have seen others, frightened at his own shadow. This was probably owing to his having been effectually conquered and his spirits broken.

After the boats were armed, I ordered the men to get into them, and they obeyed with cheerfulness. I was going myself, but Don Bonito took hold of my hand and forbade me, saying, you have saved my life, and now you are going to throw away your own. Some of my confidential officers asked me if it would be prudent for me to go, and leave the Perseverance in such an unguarded state; and also, if any thing should happen to me, what would be the consequence to the voyage. Every man on board, they observed, would willingly go, if it were my pleasure. I gave their remonstrances a moment's consideration, and felt their weight. I then ordered into the boats my chief officer, Mr. Low, who commanded the party; and under him, Mr. Brown, my second officer, my brother William, Mr. George Russell, son

to major Benjamin Russell of Boston, and Mr. Nathaniel Luther, midshipmen; William Clark, boatswain; Charles Spence, gunner; and thirteen seamen. By way of encouragement, I told them that Don Bonito considered
the ship and what was in her as lost; that the value was more than one hundred thousand dollars; that if we would take her, it should be all our own;
and that if we should afterwards be disposed to give him up one half, it
would be considered as a present. I likewise reminded them of the suffering condition of the poor Spaniards remaining on board, whom I then saw
with my spy-glass as high aloft as they could get on the top-gallant-masts,
and knowing that death must be their fate if they came down. I told them,
never to see my face again, if they did not take her; and these were all of
them pretty powerful stimulants. I wished God to prosper them in the discharge of their arduous duty, and they shoved off. They pulled after and
came up with the Tryal, took their station upon each quarter, and commenced a brisk fire of musketry, directing it as much at the man at the
helm as they could, as that was likewise a place of resort for the negroes.
At length they drove the chief mate from it, who had been compelled to
steer the ship. He ran up the miz[z]en rigging as high as the cross jack
yard, and called out in Spanish, "Don't board." This induced our people to
believe that he favoured the cause of the negroes; they fired at him, and
two balls took effect; one of them went through his side, but did not go
deep enough to be mortal; and the other went through one of his thighs.
This brought him down on deck again. They found the ship made such
head way, that the boats could hardly keep up with her, as the breeze was
growing stronger. They then called to the Spaniards, who were still as high
aloft as they could get, to come down on the yards, and cut away the rob-
ings and earings of the topsails, and let them fall from the yards, so that
they might not hold any wind. They accordingly did so. About the same time,
the Spaniard who was steering the ship, was killed; (he is sometimes called
passenger and sometimes *clerk*, in the different depositions,) so that both
these circumstances combined, rendered her unmanageable by such people
as were left on board. She came round to the wind, and both boats boarded,
one on each bow, when she was carried by hard fighting. The negroes
defended themselves with desperate courage; and after our people had
boarded them, they found they had barricadoed the deck by making a breast
work of the water casks which we had left on board, and sacks of matta
[mate], abreast the mainmast, from one side of the ship to the other, to the
height of six feet; behind which they defended themselves with all the
means in their power to the last; and our people had to force their way over
this breast work before they could compel them to surrender. The other

parts of the transaction have some of them been, and the remainder will be hereafter stated.

On going on board the next morning with hand-cuffs, leg-irons, and shackled bolts, to secure the hands and feet of the negroes, the sight which presented itself to our view was truly horrid. They had got all the men who were living made fast, hands and feet, to the ring bolts in the deck; some of them had parts of their bowels hanging out, and some with half their backs and thighs shaved off. This was done with our boarding lances, which were always kept exceedingly sharp, and as bright as a gentleman's sword. Whilst putting them in irons, I had to exercise as much authority over the Spanish captain and his crew, as I had to use over my own men on any other occasion, to prevent them from cutting to pieces and killing these poor unfortunate beings. I observed one of the Spanish sailors had found a razor in the pocket of an old jacket of his, which one of the slaves had on; he opened it, and made a cut upon the negro's head. He seemed to aim at his throat, and it bled shockingly. Seeing several more about to engage in the same kind of barbarity, I commanded them not to hurt another of them, on pain of being brought to the gang-way and flogged. The captain also, I noticed, had a dirk, which he had secreted at the time the negroes were massacreing the Spaniards. I did not observe, however, that he intended to use it, until one of my people gave me a twitch by the elbow, to draw my attention to what was passing, when I saw him in the act of stabbing one of the slaves. I immediately caught hold of him, took away his dirk, and threatened him with the consequences of my displeasure, if he attempted to hurt one of them. Thus I was obliged to be continually vigilant, to prevent them from using violence towards these wretched creatures.

After we had put every thing in order on board the Spanish ship, and swept for and obtained her anchors, which the negroes had cut her from, we sailed on the 23d, both ships in company, for Conception, where we anchored on the 26th. After the common forms were passed, we delivered the ship, and all that was on board her, to the captain, whom we had befriended. We delivered him also a bag of doubloons, containing, I presume, nearly a thousand; several bags of dollars, containing a like number; and several baskets of watches, some gold, and some silver: all of which had been brought on board the Perseverance for safe keeping. We detained no part of this treasure to reward us for the services we had rendered: – all that we received was faithfully returned.

After our arrival at Conception, I was mortified and very much hurt at the treatment which I received from Don Benito Cereno; but had this been the only time that I ever was treated with ingratitude, injustice, or want of compassion, I would not complain. I will only name one act of his towards me at this place. He went to the prison and took the depositions of five of my Botany bay convicts, who had left us at St. Maria, and were now in prison here. This was done by him with a view to injure my character, so that he might not be obliged to make us any compensation for what we had done for him. I never made any demand of, nor claimed in any way whatever, more than that they should give me justice; and did not ask to be my own judge, but to refer it to government. Amongst those who swore against me were the three outlawed convicts, who have been before mentioned. I had been the means, undoubtedly, of saving every one of their lives, and had supplied them with clothes. They swore every thing against me they could to effect my ruin. Amongst other atrocities, they swore I was a pirate, and made several statements that would operate equally to my disadvantage had they been believed; all of which were brought before the viceroy of Lima against me. When we met at that place, the viceroy was too great and too good a man to be misled by these false representations. He told Don Bonito, that my conduct towards him proved the injustice of these depositions, taking his own official declaration at Conception for the proof of it; that he had been informed by Don Juan Calminaries, who was commandant of the marine, and was at that time, and after the affair of the Tryal, on the coast of Chili; that Calminaries had informed him how both Don Bonito and myself had conducted, and he was satisfied that no man had behaved better, under all circumstances, than the American captain had done to Don Bonito, and that he never had seen or heard of any man treating another with so much dishonesty and ingratitude as he had treated the American. The viceroy had previously issued an order, on his own authority, to Don Bonito, to deliver to me eight thousand dollars as part payment for services rendered him. This order was not given till his Excellency had consulted all the tribunals holding jurisdiction over similar cases, except the twelve royal judges. These judges exercise a supreme authority over all the courts in Peru, and reserve to themselves the right of giving a final decision in all questions of law. Whenever either party is dissatisfied with the decision of the inferior courts in this kingdom, they have a right of appeal to the twelve judges. Don Bonito had attempted an appeal from the viceroy's order to the royal judges. The viceroy sent for me, and acquainted me of Don Bonito's attempt; at the same time recommending to me to accede to it, as the royal judges well understood the nature of the business, and would do much better for me than his order would. He observed at the same time, that they were men of too great characters to be biassed or swayed from doing justice by any party; they holding their appointments immediately from his majesty. He said, if I requested it, Don Bonito should be holden to his order. I then represented, that I had been in Lima nearly two months, waiting for different tribunals, to satisfy his Excellency what was safe for him, and best to be done for me, short of a course of law, which I was neither able nor willing to enter into; that I had then nearly thirty men on different islands, and on board my tender, which was then somewhere amongst the islands on the coast of Chili; that they had no method that I knew of to help themselves, or receive succor, except from me; and that if I was to defer the time any longer it amounted to a certainty, that they must suffer. I therefore must pray that his Excellency's order might be put in force.

Don Bonito, who was owner of the ship and part of the cargo, had been quibbling and using all his endeavors to delay the time of payment, provided the appeal was not allowed, when his Excellency told him to get out of his sight, that he would pay the money himself, and put him (Don Bonito) into a dungeon, where he should not see sun, moon, or stars; and was about giving the order, when a very respectable company of merchants waited on him and pleaded for Don Bonito; praying that his Excellency would favour him on account of his family, who were very rich and respectable. The viceroy remarked that Don Bonito's character had been such as to disgrace any family, that had any pretensions to respectability; but that he should grant their prayer, provided there was no more reason for complaint. The last transaction brought me the money in two hours; by which time I was extremely distressed, enought, I believe, to have punished me for a great many of my bad deeds.

When I take a retrospective view of my life, I cannot find in my soul, that I ever have done any thing to deserve such misery and ingratitude as I have suffered at different periods, and in general, from the very persons to whom I have rendered the greatest services.

The following Documents were officially translated, and are inserted without alteration, from the original papers. This I thought to be the most correct course, as it would give the reader a better view of the subject than any other method that could be adopted. My deposition and that of Mr. Luther, were communicated through a bad linguist, who could not speak the English language so well as I could the Spanish, Mr. Luther not having any knowledge of the Spanish language. The Spanish captain's deposition, together with Mr. Luther's and my own, were translated into English again, as now inserted; having thus undergone two translations. These circumstances, will, we hope, be a sufficient apology for any thing which may appear to the reader not to be perfectly consistent, one declaration with another; and for any impropriety of expression.

Official Documents.

STAMP.   A FAITHFUL TRANSLATION OF THE DEPOSITIONS
OF DON BENITO CERENO, OF DON AMASA DELANO,
AND OF DON NATHANIEL LUTHER, TOGETHER WITH
THE DOCUMENTS OF THE COMMENCEMENT OF
THE PROCESS, UNDER THE KING'S SEAL.

I DON JOSE DE ABOS, and Padilla, his Majesty's Notary for the Royal Revenue, and Register of this Province, and Notary Public of the Holy Crusade of this Bishoprick, &c.

Do certify and declare, as much as requisite in law, that, in the criminal cause, which by an order of the Royal Justice, Doctor DON JUAN MARTINEZ DE ROZAS, deputy assessor general of this province, conducted against the Senegal Negroes, that the ship Tryal was carrying from the port of Valparaiso, to that of Callao of Lima, in the month of December last. There is at the beginning of the prosecution, a decree in continuation of the declaration of her captain, Don Benito Cereno, and on the back of the twenty-sixth leaf, that of the captain of the American ship, the Perseverance, Amasa Delano; and that of the supercargo of this ship, Nathaniel Luther, midshipman, of the United States, on the thirtieth leaf; as also the Sentence of the aforesaid cause, on the back of the 72d leaf; and the confirmation of the Royal Audience, of this District, on the 78th and 79th leaves; and an official order of the Tribunal with which the cause and every thing else therein continued, is remitted back; which proceedings with a representation made by the said American captain, Amasa Delano, to this Intendency, against the Spanish captain of the ship Tryal, Don Benito Cereno, and answers thereto – are in the following manner –

Decree of the Commencement of the Process.

In the port of Talcahuane, the twenty-fourth of the month of February, one thousand eight hundred and five, Doctor Don Juan Martinez de Rozas, Counsellor of the Royal Audience of this Kingdom, Deputy Assessor, and learned in the law, of this Intendency, having the deputation thereof on account of the absence of his Lordship, the Governor Intendent – Said, that whereas the ship Tryal, has just cast anchor in the road of this port, and her captain, Don Benito Cereno, has made the declaration of the twentieth of December, he sailed from the port of Valparaiso, bound to that of Callao; having his ship loaded with produce and merchandize of the country, with sixty-three negroes of all sexes and ages, and besides nine sucking infants; that the twenty-sixth, in the night, revolted, killed eighteen of his men, and made themselves master of the ship – that afterwards they killed seven men more, and obliged him to carry them to the coast of Africa, at Senegal, of which they were natives; that Tuesday the nineteenth, he put into the island of Santa Maria, for the purpose of taking in water, and he found in its harbour the American ship, the Perseverance, commanded by captain Amasa Delano, who being informed of the revolt of the negroes on board the ship Tryal, killed five or six of them in the engagement, and finally overcame them; that the ship being recovered, he supplied him with hands, and brought him to the port. – Wherefore, for examining the truth of these facts, and inflict on the guilty of such heinous crimes, the penalties provided by law. He therefore orders that this decree commencing the process, should be extended, that agreeably to its tenor, the witnesses, that should be able to give an account of them, be examined – thus ordered by his honour, which I attest. – Doctor ROZAS

Before me, JOSE DE ABOS, and Padilla, his Majesty's Notary of Royal Revenue and Registers.

Declaration of first Witness, DON BENITO CERENO.

The same day and month and year, his Honour ordered the captain of the ship Tryal, Don Benito Cereno, to appear, of whom he received before me, the oath, which he took by God, our Lord, and a Sign of the Cross, under which he promised to tell the truth of whatever he should know and should be asked – and being interrogated agreeably to the tenor of the act, commencing the process, he said, that the twentieth of December last, he set sail with his ship from the port of Valparaiso, bound to that of Callao; loaded with the produce of the country, and seventy-two negroes of both sexes, and of all ages, belonging to Don Alexandro Aranda, inhabitant of the city of Mendosa; that the crew of the ship consisted of thirty-six men, besides the persons who went [as] passengers; that the negroes were of the following ages, – twenty from twelve to sixteen years, one from about eighteen to nineteen years, named Jose, and this was the man that waited upon his master Don Alexandro, who speaks well the Spanish, having had him four or five years; a mulatto, named Francisco, native of the province of Buenos Ayres, aged about thirty-five years; a smart negro, named Joaquin, who had been for many years among the Spaniards, aged twenty six years, and a caulker by trade; twelve full grown negroes, aged from twenty-five to fifty years, all raw and born on the coast of Senegal – whose names are as follow, – the first was named Babo, and he was killed, – the second who is his son, is named Muri, – the third, Matiluqui, – the fourth, Yola, – the fifth, Yau, – the sixth Atufal, who was killed, – the seventh, Diamelo, also killed, – the eighth, Lecbe, likewise killed, – the ninth, Natu, in the same manner killed, and that he does not recollect the names of the others; but that he will take due account of them all, and remit to the court; and twenty-eight women of all ages; – that all the negroes slept upon deck, as is customary in this navigation; and none wore fetters, because the owner, Aranda told him that they were all tractable; that the twenty-seventh of December, at three o'clock in the morning, all the Spaniards being asleep except the two officers on the watch, who were the boatswain Juan Robles, and the carpenter Juan Balltista Gayete, and the helmsman and his boy; the negroes revolted suddenly, wounded dangerously the boatswain and the carpenter, and successively killed eighteen men of those who were sleeping upon deck, – some with sticks and daggers, and others by throwing them alive overboard, after tying them; that of the Spaniards who were upon deck, they left about seven, as he thinks, alive and tied, to manœuvre the ship; and three or four more who hid themselves, remained also alive, although in the act of revolt, they made themselves masters of the hatchway, six or seven wounded, went through it to the cock-pit without any hindrance on their part; that in the act of revolt, the mate and another person, whose name he does not recollect, attempted to come up through the hatchway, but having been wounded at the onset, they were obliged to return to the cabin; that the deponent resolved at break of day to come up the companion-way, where the negro Babo was, being the ring leader, and another who assisted him, and having spoken to them, exhorted them to cease committing such atrocities – asking them at the same time what they wanted and intended to do – offering himself to obey their commands; that notwithstanding this, they threw, in his presence, three men, alive and tied, overboard; that they told the deponent to come up, and that they would not kill him – which having done, they asked him whether there were in these seas any negro countries, where they might be carried, and he answered them, no; that they afterwards told him to carry them to Senegal, or to the neighbouring islands of St. Nicolas – and he answered them, that this was impossible, on account of the great distance, the bad condition of the vessel, the want of provisions, sails and water; that they replied to him, he must carry them in any way; that they would do and conform themselves to every thing the deponent should require as to eating and drinking, that after a long conference, being absolutely compelled to please them, for they threatened him to kill them all, if they were not at all events carried to Senegal. He told them that what was most wanting for the voyage was water; that they would go near the coast to take it, and thence they would proceed on their course – that the negroes agreed to it; and the deponent steered towards the intermediate ports, hoping to meet some Spanish or foreign vessel that would save them; that within ten or eleven days they saw the land, and continued their course by it in the vicinity of Nasca; that the deponent observed that the negroes were now restless, and mutinous, because he did not effect the taking in of water, they having required with threats that it should be done, without fail the following day; he told them they saw plainly that the coast was steep, and the rivers designated in the maps were not to be found, with other reasons suitable to the circumstances; that the best way would be to go to the island of Santa Maria, where they might water and victual easily, it being a desert island, as the foreigners did; that the deponent did not go to Pisco, that was near, nor make any other port of the coast, because the negroes had intimated to him several times, that they would kill them all the very moment they should perceive any city, town, or settlement, on the shores to which they should be carried; that having determined to go to the island of Santa Maria, as the deponent had planned, for the purpose of trying whether in the passage or in the island itself, they could find any vessel that should favour them, or whether he could escape from it in a boat to the neighbouring coast of Arruco. To adopt the necessary means he immediately changed his course, steering for the island; that the negroes held daily conferences, in which they discussed what was necessary for their design of returning to Senegal, whether they were to kill all the Spaniards, and particularly the deponent; that eight days after parting from the coast of Nasca, the deponent being on the watch a little after day-break, and soon after the negroes had their meeting, the negro Mure came to the place where the deponent was, and told him, that his comrades had determined to kill his master, Don Alexandro Aranda, because they said they could not otherwise obtain their liberty, and that he should call the mate, who was sleeping, before they executed it, for fear, as he understood, that he should not be killed with the rest; that the deponent prayed and told him all that was necessary in such a circumstance to dissuade him from his design, but all was useless, for the negro Mure answered him, that the thing could not be prevented, and that they should all run the risk of being killed if they should attempt to dissuade or obstruct them in the act; that in this conflict the deponent called the mate, and immediately the negro Mure ordered the negro Matinqui, and another named Lecbe, who died in the island of Santa Maria, to go and commit this murder; that the two negroes went down to the birth of Don Alexandro, and stabbed him in his bed; that yet half alive and agonizing, they dragged him on deck and threw him overboard; that the clerk, Don Lorenzo Bargas, was sleeping in the opposite birth [berth], and awaking at the cries of Aranda, surprised by them, and at the sight of the negroes, who had bloody daggers in their hands, he threw himself into the sea through a window which was near him, and was miserably drowned, without being in the power of the deponent to assist, or take him up, though he immediately put out his boat; that a short time after killing Aranda, they got upon deck his german-cousin, Don Francisco Masa, and his other clerk, called Don Hermenegildo, a native of Spain, and a relation of the said Aranda, besides the boatswain, Juan Robles, the boatswain's mate, Manuel Viseaya, and two or three others of the sailors, all of whom were wounded, and having stabbed them again, they threw them alive into the sea, although they made no resistance, nor begged for any thing else but mercy; that the boatswain, Juan Robles, who knew how to swim, kept himself the longest above water, making acts of contrition, and in the last words he uttered, charged this deponent to cause mass to be said for his soul, to our Lady of Succour; that having finished this slaughter, the negro Mure told him that they had now done all, and that he might pursue his destination, warning him that they would kill all the Spaniards, if they saw them speak, or plot any thing against them – a threat which they repeated almost every day; that before this occurrence last mentioned, they had tied the cook to throw him overboard for I know not what thing they heard him speak, and finally they spared his life at the request of the deponent; that a few days after, the deponent endeavoured not to omit any means to preserve their lives – spoke to them peace and tranquillity, and agreed to draw up a paper, signed by the deponent, and the sailors who could write, as also by the negroes, Babo and Atufal, who could do it in their language, though they were new, in which he obliged himself to carry them to Senegal, and they not to kill any more, and to return to them the ship with the cargo, with which they were for that satisfied and quieted; that omitting other events which daily happened, and which can only serve to recal[l] their past misfortunes and conflicts, after forty-two days navigation, reckoned from the time they sailed from Nasca, during which they navigated under a scanty allowance of water, they at last arrived at the island of Santa Maria, on Tuesday the nineteenth instant, at about five o'clock in the afternoon, at which hour they cast anchor very near the American ship Perseverance, which lay in the same port, commanded by the *generous captain Amasa Delano,* but at seven o'clock in the morning they had already descried the port, and the negroes became uneasy as soon as they saw the ship, and the deponent, to appease and quiet them, proposed to them to say and do all that he will declare to have said to the American captain, with which they were tranquilized warning him that if he varied in the least, or uttered any word that should give the least intimation of the past occurrences, they would instantly kill him and all his companions; that about eight o'clock in the morning, captain Amasa Delano came in his boat, on board the Tryal, and all gladly received him; that the deponent, acting then the part of an owner and a free captain of the ship, told them that he came from Buenos Ayres, bound to Lima, with that parcel of negroes; that at the cape many had died, that also, all the sea officers and the greatest part of the crew had died, there remained to him no other sailors than these few who were in sight, and that for want of them the sails had been torn to pieces; that the heavy storms off the cape had obliged them to throw overboard the greatest part of the cargo, and the water pipes; that consequently he had no more water; that he had thought of putting into the port of Conception, but that the north wind had prevented him, as also the want of water, for he had only enough for that day, concluded by asking of him supplies; – that the *generous captain Amasa Delano* immediately offered them sails, pipes, and whatever he wanted, to pursue his voyage to Lima, without entering any other port, leaving it to his pleasure to refund him for these supplies at Callao, or pay him for them if he thought best; that he immediately ordered his boat for the purpose of bringing him water, sugar, and bread, as they did; that Amasa Delano remained on board the Tryal all the day, till he left the ship anchored at five o'clock in the afternoon, deponent speaking to him always of his pretended misfortunes, under the fore-mentioned principles, without having had it in his power to tell a single word, nor giving him the least hint, that he might know the truth, and state of things; because the negro Mure, who is a man of capacity and talents, performing the office of an officious servant, with all the appearance of submission of the humble slave, did not leave the deponent one moment, in order to observe his actions and words; for he understands well the Spanish, and besides there were thereabout some others who were constantly on the watch and understood it also; that a moment in which Amasa Delano left the deponent, Mure asked him, how do we come on? and the deponent answered them, well; he gives us all the supplies we want, but he asked him afterwards how many men he had, and the deponent told him that he had thirty men; but that twenty of them were on the island, and there were in the vessel only those whom he saw there in the two boats; and then the negro told him, well, you will be the captain of this ship to night and his also, for three negroes are sufficient to take it; that as soon as they had cast anchor, at five of the clock, as has been stated, the American captain took leave, to return to his vessel, and the deponent accompanied him as far as the gunwale, where he staid under pretence of taking leave, until he should have got into his boat; but on shoving off, the deponent jumped from the gunwale into the boat and fell into it, without knowing how, and without sustaining, fortunately, any harm; but he immediately hallooed to the Spaniards in the ship, "Overboard, those that can swim, the rest to the rigging." That he instantly told the captain, by means of the Portuguese interpreter, that they were revolted negroes, who had killed all his people; that the said captain soon understood the affair, and recovered from his surprise, which the leap of the deponent occasioned, and told him, "Be not afraid, be not afraid, set down and be easy," and ordered his sailors to row towards his ship, and before coming up to her, he hailed, to get a cannon ready and run it out of the port hole, which they did very quick, and fired with it a few shots at the negroes; that in the mean while the boat was sent to pick up two men who had thrown themselves overboard, which they effected; that the negroes cut the cables, and endeavoured to sail away; that Amasa Delano, seeing them sailing away, and the cannon could not subdue them, ordered his people to get muskets, pikes, and sabres ready, and all his men offered themselves willingly to board them with the boats; that captain Amasa Delano wanted to go in person, and was going to embark the first, but the deponent prevented him, and after many entreaties he finally remained, saying, though that circumstance would procure him much honour, he would stay to please him, and keep him company in his affliction, and would send a brother of his, on whom he said he placed as much reliance as on himself; his brother, the mates, and eighteen men, whom he had in his vessel, embarked in the two boats, and made their way towards the Tryal, which was already under sail; that they rowed considerably in pursuing the ship, and kept up a musketry fire; but that they could not overtake them, until they hallooed to the sailors on the rigging, to unbend or take away the sails, which they accordingly did, letting them fall on the deck; that they were then able to lay themselves alongside, keeping up constantly a musketry fire, whilst some got up the sides on deck, with pikes and sabres, and the others remained in the stern of the boat, keeping up also a fire, until they got up finally by the same side, and engaged the negroes, who defended themselves to the last with their weapons, rushing upon the points of the pikes with an extraordinary fury; that the Americans killed five or six negroes, and these were Babo, Atufal, Dick, Natu, Qiamolo, and does not recollect any other; that they wounded several others, and at last conquered and made them prisoners; that at ten o'clock at night, the first mate with three men, came to inform the captain that the ship had been taken, and came also for the purpose of being cured of a dangerous wound, made by a point of a dagger, which he had received in his breast; that two other Americans had been slightly wounded; the captain left nine men to take care of the ship as far as this port; he accompanied her with his own until both ships, the Tryal and Perseverance, cast anchor between nine and eleven o'clock in the forenoon of this day; that the deponent has not seen the twenty negroes, from twelve to sixteen years of age, have any share in the execution of the murders; nor does he believe they have had, on account of their age, although all were knowing to the insurrection; that the negro Jose, eighteen years old, and in the service of Don Alexandro, was the one who communicated the information to the negro Mure and his comrades, of the state of things before the revolt; and this is known, because in the preceding nights he used to come to sleep from below, where they were, and had secret conversations with Mure, in which he was seen several times by the mate; and one night he drove him away twice; that this same negro Jose, was the one who advised the other negroes to kill his master, Don Alexandro; and that this is known, because the negroes have said it; that on the first revolt, the negro Jose was upon deck with the other revolted negroes, but it is not known whether he materially participated in the murders; that the mulatto Francisco was of the band of revolters, and one of their number; that the negro Joaquin was also one of the worst of them, for that on the day the ship was taken, he assisted in the defence of her with a hatchet in one hand and a dagger in the other, as the sailors told him; that in sight of the deponent, he stabbed Don Francisco Masa, when he was carrying him to throw him overboard alive, he being the one who held him fast; that the twelve or thirteen negroes, from twenty-five to fifty years of age, were with the former, the principal revolters, and committed the murders and atrocities before related; that five or six of them were killed, as has been said, in the attack on the ship, and the following remained alive and are prisoners, – to wit – Mure, who acted as captain and commander of them, and on all the insurrections and posterior events, Matinqui, Alathano, Yau, Luis, Mapenda, Yola, Yambaio, being eight in number, and with Jose, Joaquin, and Francisco, who are also alive, making the member of eleven of the remaining insurgents; that the negresses of age, were knowing to the revolt, and influenced the death of their master; who also used their influence to kill the deponent; that in the act of murder, and before that of the engagement of the ship, they began to sing, and were singing a very melancholy song during the action, to excite the courage of the negroes; that the statement he has just given of the negroes who are alive, has been made by the officers of the ship; that of the thirty-six men of the crew and passengers, which the deponent had knowledge of, twelve only including the mate remained alive, besides four cabin boys, who were not included in that number; that they broke an arm of one of those cabin boys, named Francisco Raneds, and gave him three or four stabs, which are already healed; that in the engagement of the ship, the second clerk, Don Jose Morairi, was killed by a musket ball fired at him through accident, for having incautiously presented himself on the gunwale; that at the time of the attack of the ship, Don Joaquin Arambaolaza was on one of the yards flying from the negroes, and at the approach of the boats, he hallooed by order of the negroes, not to board, on which account the Americans thought he was also one of the revolters, and fired two balls at him, one passed through one of his thighs, and the other in the chest of his body, of which he is now confined, though the American captain, who has him on board, says he will recover; that in order to be able to proceed from the coast of Nasca, to the island of Santa Maria, he saw himself obliged to lighten the ship, by throwing more than one third of the cargo overboard, for he could not have made that voyage otherwise; that what he has said is the most substantial of what occurs to him on this unfortunate event, and the truth, under the oath that he has taken, — which declaration he affirmed and ratified, after hearing it read to him. He said that he was twenty-nine years of age; — and signed with his honour — which I certify.

BENITO CERENO.

DOCTOR ROZAS
Before me. – PADILLA.

RATIFICATION.

In the port of Talcahuano, the first day of the month of March, in the year one thousand eight hundred and five, – the same Honourable Judge of this cause caused to appear in his presence the captain of the ship Tryal, Don Benito Cereno, of whom he received an oath, before me, which he took conformably to law, under which he promised to tell the truth of what he should know, and of what he should be asked, and having read to him the foregoing declaration, and being asked if it is the same he has given and whether he has to add or to take off any thing, – he said, that it is the same he has given, that he affirms and ratifies it; and has only to add, that the new negroes were thirteen, and the females comprehended twenty-seven, without including the infants, and that one of them died from hunger or thi[r]st, and two young negroes of those from twelve to sixteen, together with an infant. And he signed it with his honour – which I certify.

BENITO CERENO.

DOCTOR ROZAS.
   Before me. – PADILLA.

DECLARATION OF DOM AMASA DELANO.

The same day, month and year, his Honour, ordered the captain of the American ship Perseverance to appear, whose oath his Honour received, which he took by placing his right hand on the Evangelists, under which he promised to tell the truth of what he should know and be asked – and being interrogated according to the decree, beginning this process, through the medium of the interpreter Carlos Elli, who likewise swore to exercise well and lawfully his office, that the nineteenth or twentieth of the month, as he believes, agreeably to the calculation he keeps from the eastward, being at the island of Santa Maria, at anchor, he descried at seven o'clock in the morning, a ship coming round the point; that he asked his crew what ship that was; they replied that they did not know her; that taking his spy-glass he perceived she bore no colours; that he took his barge, and his net for fishing, and went on board of her, that when he got on deck he embraced the Spanish captain, who told him that he had been four months and twenty six days from Buenoes Ayres; that many of his people had died of the scurvy, and that he was in great want of supplies – particularly pipes for water, duck for sails, and refreshment for his crew; that the deponent offered to give and supply him with every thing he asked and wanted; that the Spanish captain did nothing else, because the ring-leader of the negroes was constantly at their elbows, observing what was said. That immediately he sent his barge to his own ship to bring, (as they accordingly did) water, peas, bread, sugar, and fish. That he also sent for his long boat to bring a load of water, and having brought it, he returned to his own ship; that in parting he asked the Spanish captain to come on board his ship to take coffee, tea, and other refreshments; but he answered him with coldness and indifference; that he could not go then, but that he would in two or three days. That at the same time he visited him, the ship Tryal cast anchor in the port, about four o'clock in the afternoon, – that he told his people belonging to his boat to embark in order to return to his ship, that the deponent also left the deck to get into his barge, – that on getting into the barge, the Spanish captain took him by the hand and immediately gave a jump on board his boat, – that he then told him that the negroes of the Tryal had taken her, and had murdered twenty-five men, which the deponent was informed of through the medium of an interpreter, who was with him, and a Portuguese; that two or three other Spaniards threw themselves into the water, who were picked up by his boats; that he immediately went to his ship, and before reaching her, called to the mate to prepare and load the guns; that having got on board, he fired at them with his cannon, and this same deponent pointed six shots at the time the negroes of the Tryal were cutting away the cables and setting sail; that the Spanish captain told him that the ship was already going away, and that she could not be taken; that the deponent replied that he would take her; then the Spanish captain told him that if he took her, one half of her value would be his, and the other half would remain to the real owners; that thereupon he ordered the people belonging to his crew, to embark in the two boats, armed with knives, pistols, sabres, and pikes, to pursue her, and board her; that the two boats were firing at her near an hour with musketry, and at the end boarded and captured her; and that before sending his boats, he told his crew, in order to encourage them, that the Spanish captain offered to give them the half of the value of the Tryal if they took her. That having taken the ship, they came to anchor at about two o'clock in the morning very near the deponent's, leaving in her about twenty of his men; that his first mate received a very dangerous wound in his breast made with a pike, of which he lies very ill; that three other sailors were also wounded with clubs, though not dangerously; that five or six of the negroes were killed in boarding; that at six o'clock in the morning, he went with the Spanish captain on board the Tryal, to carry manacles and fetters from his ship, ordering them to be put on the negroes who remained alive, he dressed the wounded, and [accompanied] the Tryal to the anchoring ground; and in it he delivered her up manned from his crew; for until that moment he remained in possession of her; that what he has said is what he knows, and the truth, under the oath he has taken, which he affirmed and ratified after the said declaration had been read to him, – saying he was forty-two years of age, – the interpreter did not sign it because he said he did not know how – the captain signed it with his honour – which I certify.

AMASA DELANO.

DOCTOR ROZAS.
Before me. – PADILLA.

RATIFICATION.

The said day, month and year, his Honour ordered the captain of the American ship, Don Amasa Delano to appear, of whom his Honour received an oath, which he took by placing his hand on the Evangelists, under which he promised to tell the truth of what he should know, and be asked, and having read to him the foregoing declaration, through the medium of the interpreter, Ambrosio Fernandez, who likewise took an oath to exercise well and faithfully his office, – he said that he affirms and ratifies the same; that he has nothing to add or diminish, and he signed it, with his Honour, and likewise the Interpreter.

AMASA DELANO.
AMBROSIO FERNANDEZ.

Doctor ROZAS.
Before me. – PADILLA.

DECLARATION OF DON NATHANIEL LUTHER, MIDSHIPMAN.

The same day, month and year, his Honour ordered Don Nathaniel Luther, first midshipman of the American ship Perseverance, and acting as clerk to the captain, to appear, of whom he received an oath, and which he took by placing his right hand on the Evangelists, under which he promised to tell the truth of what he should know and be asked, and being interrogated agreeably to the decree commencing this process, through the medium of the Interpreter Carlos Elli, he said that the deponent himself was one that boarded, and helped to take the ship Tryal in the boats; that he knows that his captain, Amasa Delano, has deposed on every thing that happened in this affair; that in order to avoid delay he requests that his declaration should be read to him, and he will tell whether it is conformable to the happening of the events; that if anything should be omitted he will observe it, and add to it, doing the same if he erred in any part thereof; and his Honour having acquiesced in this proposal, the Declaration made this day by captain Amasa Delano, was read to him through the medium of the Interpreter, and said, that the deponent went with his captain, Amasa Delano, to the ship Tryal, as soon as she appeared at the point of the island, which was about seven o'clock in the morning, and remained with him on board of her, until she cast anchor; that the deponent was one of those who boarded the ship Tryal in the boats, and by this he knows that the narration which the captain has made in the deposition which has been read to him, is certain and exact in all its parts; and he has only three things to add: the first, that whilst his captain remained on board the Tryal, a negro stood constantly at his elbow, and by the side of the deponent, the second, that the deponent was in the boat, when the Spanish captain jumped into it, and when the Portuguese declared that the negroes had revolted; the third, that the number of killed was six, five negroes and a Spanish sailor; that what he has said is the truth, under the oath which he has taken; which he affirmed and ratified, after his Declaration had been read to him; he said he was twenty one years of age, and signed it with his Honour, but the Interpreter did not sign it, because he said he did not know how – which I certify.

NATHANIEL LUTHER.

DOCTOR ROZAS.

Before me. – PADILLA.

RATIFICATION.

The aforesaid day, month and year, his Honour, ordered Don Nathaniel Luther, first midshipman of the American ship Perseverance, and acting as clerk to the captain, to whom he administ[e]red an oath, which he took by placing his hand on the Evangelists, under the sanctity of which he promised to tell the truth of what he should know and be asked; and the foregoing Declaration having been read to him, which he thoroughly understood, through the medium of the Interpreter, Ambrosio Fernandez, to whom an oath was likewise administ[e]red, to exercise well and faithfully his office, he says that he affirms and ratifies the same, that he has nothing to add or diminish, and he signed it with his Honour, and the Interpreter, which I certify.

NATHANIEL LUTHER.
AMBROSIO FERNANDEZ.

DOCTOR ROZAS.

Before me. – PADILLA.

SENTENCE.

In this city of Conception, the second day of the month of March, of one thousand eight hundred and five, his Honour Doctor Don Juan Martinez de

Rozas, Deputy Assessor and learned in the law, of this intendency, having the execution thereof on account of the absence of his Honour, the principal having seen the proceedings, which he has conducted officially against the negroes of the ship Tryal, in consequence of the insurrection and atrocities which they have committed on board of her. – He declared, that the insurrection and revolt of said negroes, being sufficiently substantiated, with premedi[t]ated intent, the twenty seventh of December last, at three o'clock in the morning; that taking by surprise the sleeping crew, they killed eighteen men, some with sticks, and daggers, and others by throwing them alive overboard; that a few days afterward with the same deliberate intent, they stabbed their master Don Alexandro Aranda, and threw Don Franciso Masa, his german cousin, Hermenegildo, his relation, and the other wounded persons who were confined in the berths, overboard alive; that in the island of Santa Maria, they defended themselves with arms, against the Americans, who attempted to subdue them, causing the death of Don Jose Moraira the second clerk, as they had done that of the first, Don Lorenzo Bargas; the whole being considered, and the consequent guilts resulting from those heinous and atrocious actions as an example to others, he ought and did condemn the negroes, Mure, Martinqui, Alazase, Yola, Joaquin, Luis, Yau, Mapenda, and Yambaio, to the common penalty of death, which shall be executed, by taking them out and dragging them from the prison, at the tail of a beast of burden, as far as the gibbet, where they shall be hung until they are dead, and to the forfeiture of all their property, if they should have any, to be applied to the Royal Treasury; that the heads of the five first be cut off after they are dead, and be fixed on a pole, in the square of the port of Talcahuano, and the corpses of all be burnt to ashes. The negresses and young negroes of the same gang shall be present at the execution, if they should be in that city at the time thereof; that he ought and did condemn likewise, the negro Jose, servant to said Don Alexandro, and Yambaio, Francisco, Rodriguez, to ten years confinement in the place of Valdivia, to work chained, on allowance and without pay, in the work of the King, and also to attend the execution of the other criminals; and judging definitively by this sentence thus pronounced and ordered by his Honour, and that the same should be executed notwithstanding the appeal, for which he declared there was no cause, but that an account of it should be previously sent to the Royal Audience of this district, for the execution thereof with the costs.

DOCTOR ROZAS.

Before me. – JOSE DE ABOS PADILLA.
His Majesty's Notary of the Royal Revenue and Registers.

CONFIRMATION OF THE SENTENCE.

SANTIAGO, *March the twenty first, of one thousand eight hundred and five.*

Having duly considered the whole, we suppose the sentence pronounced by the Deputy Assessor of the City of Conception, to whom we remit the same for its execution and fulfilment, with the official resolution, taking first an authenticated copy of the proceedings, to give an account thereof to his Majesty: and in regard to the request of the acting Notary, to the process upon the pay of his charges, he will exercise his right when and where he shall judge best. –

There are four flourishes.

Their Honours, the President, Regent, and Auditors of his Royal Audience passed the foregoing decree, and those on the Margin set their flourishes, the day of this date, the twenty first of March, one thousand eight hundred and five; – which I certify,

ROMAN.

NOTIFICATION.

The twenty third of said month, I acquainted his Honour, the King's Attorney of the foregoing decree, – which I certify,

ROMAN.

OFFICIAL RESOLUTION.

The Tribunal has resolved to manifest by this official resolve and pleasure for the exactitude, zeal and promptness which you have discovered in the cause against the revolted negroes of the ship Tryal, which process it remits to you, with the approbation of the sentence for the execution thereof, forewarning you that before its completion, you may agree with the most Illustrious Bishop, on the subject of furnishing the spiritual aids to those miserable beings, affording the same to them with all possible dispatch. – At the same time this Royal Audience has thought fit in case you should have an opportunity of speaking with the Bostonian captain, Amasa Delano, to charge you to inform him, that they will give an account to his Majesty, of the generous and benevolent conduct which he displayed in the punctual assistance that he afforded the Spanish captain of the aforesaid ship, for the suitable manifestation, publication and noticety of such a memorable event.

God preserve you many years.

SANTIAGO, *March the twenty second, of one thousand eight hundred and five.*

JOSÉ DE SANTIAGO CONCHA.

Doctor Don JUAN MARTINEZ De ROZAS,
Deputy assessor, and learned in the law, of the Intendency of Conception.

I the unde[r]signed, sworn Interpreter of languages, do certify that the foregoing translation from the Spanish original, is true.

FRANCIS SALES.

Boston, April 15th, 1808.

N.B. It is proper here to state, that the difference of two days, in the dates of the process at Talquahauno, that of the Spaniards being the 24th of February and ours the 26th, was because they dated theirs the day we anchored in the lower harbour, which was one day before we got up abreast of the port at which time we dated ours; and our coming by the way of the Cape of Good Hope, made our reckoning of time one day different from theirs.

It is also necessary to remark, that the statement in page 332, respecting Mr. Luther being supercargo, and United States midshipman, is a mistake of the linguist. He was with me, the same as Mr. George Russell, and my brother William, midshipmen of the ship Perseverance.

On my return to America in 1807, I was gratified in receiving a polite letter from the Marquis De Case Yruso, through the medium of Juan Stoughton Esq. expressing the satisfaction of his majesty, the king of Spain, on account of our conduct in capturing the Spanish ship Tryal at the island St. Maria, accompanied with a gold medal, having his majesty's likeness on one side, and on the other the inscription, Reward of Merit. The correspondence relating to that subject, I shall insert for the satisfaction of the reader. I had been assured by the president of Chili, when I was in that country, and likewise by the viceroy of Lima, that all my conduct, and the treatment I had received, should be faithfully represented to his majesty Charles IV, who most probably would do something more for me. I had reason to expect, through the medium of so many powerful friends as I had procured at different times and places, and on different occasions, that I should most likely have received something essentially to my advantage. This probably would have been the case had it not been for the unhappy catastrophe which soon after took place in Spain, by the dethronement of Charles IV, and the distracted state of the Spanish government, which followed that event.

Philadelphia, 8th September, 1806.

Sir,

His Catholic Majesty the king of Spain, my master, having been informed by the audience of Chili of your noble and generous conduct in rescuing, off the island St. Maria, the Spanish merchant ship Tryal, captain Don Benito Cereno, with the cargo of slaves, who had mutinized, and cruelly massacred the greater part of the Spaniards on board; and by humanely supplying them afterwards with water and provisions, which they were in need of, has desired me to express to you, sir, the high sense he entertains of the spirited, humane, and successful effort of yourself and the brave crew of the Perseverance, under your command, in saving the lives of his subjects thus exposed, and in token whereof, his majesty has directed me to present to you the golden medal, with his likeness, which will be handed to you by his consul in Boston. At the same time permit me, sir, to assure you I feel particular satisfaction in being the organ of the grateful sentiments of my sovereign, on an occurrence which reflects so much honour on your character.

I have the honour to be, sir,
Your obedient servant,
Marquis De CASE YRUSO.

(Signed)
Captain Amasa Delano, *of the American Ship Perseverance, Boston.*

Boston, August, 1807

Sir,

With sentiments of gratitude I acknowledge the receipt of your Excellency's much esteemed favour of September 8th, conveying to me the pleasing information of his Catholic Majesty having been informed of the conduct of myself and the crew of the Perseverance under my command. It is peculiarly gratifying to me, to receive such honours from your Excellency's sovereign, as entertaining a sense of my spirit and honour, and successful efforts of myself and crew in saving the lives of his subjects; and still more so by receiving the token of his royal favour in the present of the golden medal bearing his likeness. The services rendered off the island St. Maria were from pure motives of humanity. They shall ever be rendered his Catholic Majesty's subjects when wanted, and it is in my power to grant. Permit me, sir, to thank your Excellency for the satisfaction that you feel in being the organ of the grateful sentiments of your sovereign on this occasion, and believe me, it shall ever be my duty publicly to acknowledge the receipt of such high considerations from such a source.

I have the honour to be
Your Excellency's most obedient,
And devoted humble servant,
AMASA DELANO.

(Signed)
His Excellency the Marquis DE CASE YRUSO.

Consular Office, 30th July, 1807.

Sir,

Under date of September last, was forwarded me the enclosed letter from his Excellency the Marquis DE CASE YRUSO, his Catholic Majesty's minister plenipotentiary to the United States of America, which explains to you the purport of the commission with which I was then charged, and until now have anxiously waited for the pleasing opportunity of carrying into effect his Excellency's orders, to present to you at the same time the gold medal therein mentioned.

It will be a pleasing circumstance to that gentleman, to be informed of your safe arrival, and my punctuality in the discharge of that duty so justly owed to the best of sovereigns, under whose benignity and patronage I have the honour to subscribe myself, with great consideration, and much respect, sir,

Your obedient humble servant,
JUAN STOUGHTON,

(Signed)

Consul of his Catholic majesty,
Residing at Boston.

AMASA DELANO, ESQ.

BOSTON, AUGUST 8TH, 1807.

SIR,

I Feel particular satisfaction in acknowledging the receipt of your esteemed favour, bearing date the 30th ult. covering a letter from the Marquis DE CASE YRUSO, his Catholic Majesty's minister plenipotentiary to the United States of America, together with the gold medal bearing his Catholic Majesty's likeness.

Permit me, sir, to return my most sincere thanks for the honours I have received through your medium, as well as for the generous, friendly treatment you have shown on the occasion. I shall ever consider it one of the first honours publicly to acknowledge them as long as I live.

These services rendered his Catholic Majesty's subjects off the island St. Maria, with the men under my command, were from pure motives of humanity. The like services we will ever render, if wanted, should it be in our power.

With due respect, permit me, sir, to subscribe myself,

Your most obedient, and
Very humble servant,
AMASA DELANO.

(Signed)

To Don JUAN STOUGHTON ESQ. HIS CATHOLIC
MAJESTY'S CONSUL, RESIDING IN BOSTON.

Suggestions for Further Reading and Research

MELVILLE BIOGRAPHY began in the 1920s, when the first collected editions of his work were being printed. Raymond Weaver's *Herman Melville* (New York: Doran, 1921) and Lewis Mumford's *Herman Melville* (New York: Harcourt, 1929) initiated an intense "Melville Revival," which peaked in the 1950s with Newton Arvin's *Herman Melville* (New York: Sloane, 1950), Leon Howard's *Herman Melville: A Biography* (Berkeley: U of California P, 1951), and Jay Leyda's great compendium of letters, clippings, and reviews, *The Melville Log: A Documentary Life of Herman Melville, 1819–1891*, in two volumes (New York: Gordian, 1969). One of Melville's granddaughters, Eleanor Melville Metcalf, who fostered much of the early research, published her own biography, *Herman Melville: Cycle and Epicycle* (Cambridge: Harvard UP, 1953). A trove of family letters preserved by Melville's sister Augusta was discovered in 1983, providing new material for biographies in the late twentieth century: Laurie Robertson-Lorant's *Melville: A Biography* (New York: Clarkson Potter, 1996) and Hershel Parker's *Herman Melville: A Biography*, in two volumes (Baltimore: Johns Hopkins UP, 1996, 2002). The first twenty-first-century critical biography is Andrew Delbanco's *Melville: His World and Work* (New York: Knopf, 2005).

SOURCES AND CONTEXTS

Amasa Delano's *A Narrative of Voyages and Travels, in the Northern and Southern Hemispheres* (Boston: E. G. House, 1817), part of which is reprinted in this volume, is considered Melville's primary source for *Benito Cereno* and was identified in Harold H. Scudder's "Melville's 'Benito Cereno' and Captain Delano's Voyages" (*PMLA* 43 [1928]: 502-32). Sterling Stuckey and Joshua Leslie have filled in the history of what happened to Delano and Cereno after the revolt in "Aftermath: Captain Delano's Claim Against Benito Cereno" (*Modern Philology* 85.3 [1988]: 265-87). Lea Newman's *A Reader's Guide to the Short Stories of Herman Melville* (Boston: G. K. Hall, 1986) offers a close comparison between *Benito Cereno* and Delano's *Narrative*, as well as a thorough review of the other sources of and scholarship on the story.

The *Amistad* revolt of 1839 has received considerable attention in Carolyn Karcher's "The Riddle of the Sphinx: Melville's 'Benito Cereno' and the *Amistad* Case," in *Critical Essays on Herman Melville's 'Benito Cereno,'* edited by Robert E. Burkholder (New York: G. K. Hall, 1992). Iyunolu Folayan Osagie also gives a complete account of the *Amistad* and its place in American and African culture in *The Amistad Revolt* (Athens: U of Georgia P, 2000). Maggie Montesinos Sale's *The Slumbering Volcano: American Slave Ship Revolts and the Production of Rebellious Masculinity* (Durham: Duke UP, 1997) looks closely at the revolts on the *Amistad* and the *Creole*, as well as at *Benito Cereno* and Frederick Douglass's "The Heroic Slave."

Carolyn Karcher's *Shadow over the Promised Land: Slavery, Race, and Violence in Melville's America* (Baton Rouge: Louisiana State UP, 1980) was one of the first treatments of race and slavery in Melville's work and provides a lengthy chapter on *Benito Cereno*. Eric J. Sundquist also offers an extended treatment of *Benito Cereno* in relation to the American slave narrative and the history of slavery in *To Wake the Nations: Race in the Making of American Literature* (Cambridge: Belknap P of Harvard UP, 1993) and "*Benito Cereno* and New World Slavery," in Burkholder. Dana Nelson's *The Word in Black and White: Reading "Race" in American Literature, 1638-1867* (New York: Oxford UP, 1992) provides important contexts for thinking about race and colonialism in Melville's period. Robert K. Wallace draws a close parallel between Melville's work, including *Benito Cereno*, and the writings of Frederick Dougass in *Douglass and Melville: Anchored Together in Neighborly Style* (New Bedford: Spinner, 2005). For a thorough treatment of the publishing world and its gendered expectations in relation to narratives of slavery, see Sarah Robbins, "Gendering the History of the Antislavery Narrative: Juxtaposing *Uncle Tom's Cabin* and *Benito Cereno, Beloved* and *Middle Passage*" (*American Quarterly* 49.3 [1997]: 531-73).

Sterling Stuckey's work supplies the African background for understanding Melville's work and includes two chapters on *Benito Cereno* in *Going through the Storm: The Influence of African American Art in History* (New York: Oxford UP, 1994). He also has an important essay on what Melville might have known of African song and dance, "The Tambourine in Glory: African Culture and Melville's Art," in *The Cambridge Companion to Herman Melville*, edited by Robert S. Levine (Cambridge: Cambridge UP, 1998).

Rosalie Feltenstein's "Melville's 'Benito Cereno'" (*American Literature* 19 [1947]: 245-55) supplies considerable material on the references to Spain, the Inquisition, and monastic orders in *Benito Cereno*. On the allusion to Charles V and the role of imperial Spain in this story, H. Bruce Franklin's essay "'Apparent Symbol of Despotic Command': Melville's *Benito Cereno*," in Burkholder, is helpful. For an excellent study of Catholicism and Melville's relationship to religion, see Jenny Franchot, *Roads to Rome: The Antebellum Protestant Encounter with Catholicism* (Berkeley: U of California P, 1994).

CRITICAL STUDIES

Interest in Melville's short fiction burgeoned in the second half of the twentieth century as scholarship on his major novels, especially *Moby-Dick*, peaked. Volumes on Melville's short fiction include R. Bruce Bickley Jr.'s *The Method of Melville's Short Fiction* (Durham: Duke UP, 1975); William B. Dillingham's *Melville's Short Fiction, 1853-1856* (Athens: U of Georgia P, 1977); Marvin Fisher's *Going Under: Melville's Short Fiction and the American 1850s* (Baton Rouge: Louisiana State UP, 1977); Harold Bloom's *Herman Melville's* Billy Budd, 'Benito Cereno,' 'Bartleby the Scrivener,' *and Other Tales* (New York: Chelsea House, 1987); and Lea Newman's *A Reader's Guide to the Short Stories of Herman Melville* (Boston: G. K. Hall, 1986). Studies of *Benito Cereno* especially proliferated in the wake of the civil rights movement of the 1960s, when critics began to realize the relevance of Melville's treatments of race and slavery. For collections devoted solely to *Benito Cereno*, see Seymour L. Gross's *A Benito Cereno Handbook* (Belmont: Wadsworth, 1965) and Robert E. Burkholder's *Critical Essays on Herman Melville's 'Benito Cereno'* (New York: G. K. Hall, 1992).

A number of companions and collections offer a range of resources for studying Melville, including his short fiction: John Bryant's *A Companion to Melville Studies* (Westport: Greenwood, 1986); Robert S. Levine's *The Cambridge Companion to Herman Melville* (Cambridge: Cambridge UP, 1998); Giles Gunn's *A Historical Guide to Herman Melville* (Oxford: Oxford UP, 2005); and Wyn Kelley's *A Companion to Herman Melville* (Oxford: Blackwell, 2006).

As might be expected, much of the strongest work on *Benito Cereno* focuses on race, slavery, and colonialism. Important chapters on these issues appear in Jean Fagan Yellin's *The Intricate Knot: Black Figures in American Literature, 1776-1863* (New York: New York UP, 1972); Robert S. Levine's *Conspiracy and Romance: Studies in Brockden Brown, Cooper, Hawthorne, and Melville* (Cambridge: Cambridge UP, 1989); Leonard Cassuto's *The Inhuman Race: The Racial Grotesque in American Literature and Culture* (New York: Columbia UP, 1997); and Geoffrey Sanborn's *The Sign of the Cannibal: Melville and the Making of a Postcolonial Reader* (Durham: Duke UP, 1998).

Other themes have received attention as well, especially political and ideological issues. Useful works specifically on *Benito Cereno* include treatments of ideology and politics, such as James H. Kavanagh's "That Hive of Subtlety: 'Benito Cereno' and the Liberal Hero," in *Ideology and Classic American Literature*, edited by Sacvan Bercovitch and Myra Jehlen (Cambridge: Cambridge UP, 1986); William Bartley's "'The Creature of His Own Tasteful Hands': Herman Melville's *Benito Cereno* and the Empire of Might" (*Modern Philology* 93 [1996]: 445–67); and Maurice Lee's study of the politics of language, "Melville's Subversive Political Philosophy: 'Benito Cereno' and the Fate of Speech" (*American Literature* 72.3 [2000]: 495–519).

In general studies of Melville's work, a range of political and social issues have received attention. Some of those most relevant to a study of *Benito Cereno* include Michael Paul Rogin's *Subversive Genealogy: The Politics and Art of Herman Melville* (New York: Knopf, 1983); Sheila Post-Lauria's *Correspondent Colorings: Melville in the Marketplace* (Amherst: U of Massachusetts P, 1996); Robert K. Martin's *Hero, Captain, and Stranger: Male Friendship, Social Critique and Literary Form in the Novels of Herman Melville* (Chapel Hill: U of North Carolina P, 1986); and Samuel Otter's *Melville's Anatomies: Bodies, Discourse, and Ideology in Antebellum America* (Berkeley: U of California P, 1998).

INTERNET SITES

To visit the site of Arrowhead, Melville's home in the Berkshires, where he wrote *Benito Cereno*, go to *Herman Melville's Arrowhead*, <http://www.mobydick.org/index.html>. A digital text of *Benito Cereno* appears at *Electronic Scholarly Publishing*, <http://www.esp.org/books/melville/piazza/contents/cereno.html>. To see the original printing of *Benito Cereno* in *Putnam's Monthly Magazine*, go to *Making of America*, <http://cdl.library.cornell.edu/moa/>.

General sites on Melville include *The Life and Works of Herman Melville*, <http://www.melville.org/>, for which the bibliography is outdated and a number of the links nonfunctional. The *American Authors* site managed by Donna Campbell at Gonzaga University has a Melville page: <http://www.wsu.edu/~campbelld/amlit/melville.htm>. *The Melville Society* site offers information about their journals and conferences: <http://people.hofstra.edu/faculty/John_L_Bryant/Melville/>.

The most useful online historical source for *Benito Cereno* is Mystic Seaport's *Exploring Amistad at Mystic Seaport*, <http://amistad.mysticseaport.org/main/welcome.html>, which offers historical material on the slave revolt and in the *Discovery* section includes an excellent essay by Mary K. Bercaw Edwards, "The *Amistad* Incident: The Source of Herman Melville's *Benito Cereno* or Not?" Another site, *Herman Melville's Benito Cereno*, <http://cla.calpoly.edu/~jbattenb/benitocereno/home-bc.htm>, offers maps and a selection from Lea Newman's *A Reader's Guide to the Short Stories of Herman Melville* detailing the comparison between Delano's account of the revolt and *Benito Cereno*.

Glossary of Literary Terms

Abstract language Any language that employs intangible, nonspecific concepts. *Love, truth,* and *beauty* are abstractions. Abstract language is the opposite of concrete language. Both types have different effects and are important features of an author's style.

Allegory A narrative in which persons, objects, settings, or events represent general concepts, moral qualities, or other abstractions.

Antagonist A character in some fiction, whose motives and actions work against, or are thought to work against, those of the hero, or protagonist. The conflict between these characters shapes the plot of their story.

Archetype A term introduced in the 1930s by psychologist C. G. Jung, who described archetypes as "primordial images" repeated throughout human history. Archetypes, or archetypal patterns, recur in myths, religion, dreams,

Prepared by Beverly Lawn, Adelphi University

fantasies, and art, and are said to have power because we know them, even if unconsciously. In literature, archetypes appear in character types, plot patterns, and descriptions.

Characterization Characterization means the development of a character or characters throughout a story. Characterization includes the narrator's description of what characters look like and what they think, say, and do (these are sometimes very dissimilar). Their own actions and views of themselves, and other characters' views of and behavior toward them, are also means of characterization.

Characters One of the elements of fiction, characters are usually the people of a work of literature; characters may be animals or some other beings. Characters are those about whom a story is told and sometimes, too, the ones telling the story. Characters may be minor, or major, depending on their importance to a story.

Climax The moment of greatest intensity and conflict in the action of a story is its climax.

Concrete language Any specific, physical language that appeals to one or more of the senses – sight, hearing, taste, smell, or touch. *Stones, chairs,* and *hands* are concrete words. Concrete language is the opposite of abstract language. Both types are important features of an author's style.

Conflict Antagonism between characters, ideas, or lines of action;

between one character and the outside world; or between aspects of a character's own nature. Conflict is essential in a traditional plot.

Description Language that presents specific features of a character, object, or setting, or the details of an action or event.

Dialogue Words spoken by characters, often in the form of conversation between two or more. In stories and other forms of prose, dialogue is commonly enclosed between quotation marks. Dialogue is an important element in characterization and plot.

Diction A writer's selection of words. Particular patterns or arrangements of words in sentences and paragraphs constitute prose style. Hemingway's diction is said to be precise, concrete, and economical.

Didactic fiction A kind of fiction that is designed to present or demonstrate a moral, religious, political, or other belief or position. Didactic works are different from purely imaginative ones, which are written for their inherent interest and value. The distinction between imaginative and didactic writing is not always sharp.

Elements of fiction Major elements of fiction are plot, characters, setting, point of view, style, and theme. Skillful employment of these entities is essential in effective novels and stories. From beginning to end, each element is active and relates to the others dynamically.

Epiphany In literature, epiphany describes a sudden illumination of the significance or true meaning of a person, place, thing, idea, or situation. Often a word, gesture, or other action reveals the significance. The term was popularized by James Joyce, who explained it fully in his autobiographical novel *Stephen Hero* (written in 1914; pub. 1944).

Fiction Traditionally, a prose narrative whose plot, characters, and settings are constructions of its writer's imagination, which draws on his or her experiences and reflections. Short stories are comparatively short works of fiction, novels long ones.

Figurative language Suggestive, rather than literal, language employing metaphor, simile, or other figures of speech.

First-person narrator See point of view.

Flashback A writer's way of introducing important earlier material. As a narrator tells a story, he or she may stop the flow of events and direct the reader to an earlier time. Sometimes the reader is returned to the present, sometimes kept in the past.

Foreshadowing Words, gestures, and other actions that suggest future events or outcomes. An example would be a character's saying, "I've got a bad feeling about this," and later in the narration something "bad" does happen to the character.

Genre A type or form of literature. The major literary genres are fiction, drama, poetry, and exposition (essay or book-length biography, criticism, history, and so on). Subgenres of fiction are the novel and the short story.

Image A word or group of words evoking concrete visual, auditory, or tactile associations. An image, sometimes called a "word-picture," is an important instance of figurative language.

Interior monologue An extended speech or narrative, presumed to be thought rather than spoken by a character. Interior monologues are similar to, but different from, *stream of consciousness*, which describes mental life at the border of consciousness. Interior monologues are typically more consciously controlled and conventionally structured, however private their thoughts.

Irony A way of writing or speaking that asserts the opposite of what the author, reader, and character know to be true. *Verbal* or *rhetorical* irony accomplishes these contradictory meanings by direct misstatements. *Situational* irony is achieved when events in a narrative turn out to be very different from, or even opposite to, what is expected.

Narrative A narrator's story of characters and events over a period of time. Usually the characters can be analyzed and generally understood; usually the events proceed in a cause-and-effect relation; and usually some unity can be found among the characters, plot, point of view, style, and theme of a narrative. Novels as well as stories are usually narratives, and journalism commonly employs narrative form.

Narrator The storyteller, usually an observer who is narrating in the *third-person point of view,* or a participant in the story's action speaking in the first person. Style and tone are important clues to the nature of a narrator and the validity and objectivity of the story itself. Sometimes a narrator who takes part in the action is too emotionally involved to be trusted for objectivity or accuracy. This narrator would be called an *unreliable narrator.*

Naturalism A literary movement that began in France in the late nineteenth century, spread, moderated, and influenced much twentieth-century literature. The movement, which started in reaction against the antiscientific sentimentality of the period, borrowed from the principles, aims, and methods of scientific thinkers such as Darwin and Spencer. Early naturalists held that human lives are determined externally by society and internally by drives and instincts and that free will is an illusion. Writers were to proceed in a reporterlike, objective manner. Stephen Crane shows the influence of early naturalism, Ernest Hemingway of later, more moderate, naturalism.

Novel An extended prose narrative or work of prose fiction, usually published alone. Hawthorne's *The Scarlet Letter* is a fairly short novel, Melville's *Moby-Dick, or, the Whale* a very long one. The length of a novel enables its author to develop characters, plot, and settings in greater detail than a short story writer can.

Novella Between the short story and the novel in size and complexity. Like them, the novella is a work of prose fiction. Sometimes it is called a long short story.

Omniscient narrator See **point of view.**

Parable A simple story that illustrates a moral point or teaches a lesson. The persons, places, things, and events are connected by the moral question only. The moral position of a parable is developed through the choices of people who believe and act in certain ways and are not abstract personifications as in allegory, nor animal characters as in folk tales.

Parody Usually, a comic or satirical imitation of a serious piece of writing, exaggerating its weaknesses and ignoring its strengths. Its distinctive features are ridiculed through exaggeration and inappropriate placement in the parody.

Plot One of the elements of fiction, plot is the sequence of major events in a story, usually in a cause-effect relation. Plot and character are intimately related, since characters carry out the plot's action. Plots may be described as simple or complex, depending on their degree of complication. "Traditional" writers usually plot their stories tightly; modernist writers employ looser, often ambiguous plots.

Point of view One of the elements of fiction, point of view is the perspective, or angle of vision, from which a narrator presents a story. Point of view tells us about the narrator as well as about the characters, setting, and theme of a story. Two common points of view are *first-person narration* and *third-person narration*. If a narrator speaks of himself or herself as "I," the narration is in the first person; if the narrator's self is not apparent and the story is told about others from some distance, using "he," "she," "it," and "they," then third-person narration is likely in force. The point of view may be *omniscient* (all-knowing) or *limited.* When determining a story's point of view, it is helpful to decide whether the narrator is reporting events as they are happening or as they happened in the past; is observing or participating in the action; and is or is not emotionally involved.

Protagonist The hero or main character of a narrative or drama. The action is the presentation and resolution of the protagonist's conflict, internal or external; if the conflict is with another major character, that character is the antagonist.

Realism Literature that seeks to present life as it is really lived by real people, without didacticism or moral agendas. In the eighteenth and nineteenth centuries realism was controversial; today it is usual.

Regionalism Literature that is strongly identified with a specific place. Writers like Kate Chopin who concentrate on one area are called regional realists; writers who do so for several works are said to have strong regional elements in their body of work.

Rising action The part of a story's action that develops its conflict and leads to its climax.

Setting One of the elements of fiction, setting is the context for the action: the time, place, culture, and atmosphere in which it occurs. A work may have several settings; the relation among them may be significant to the meaning of the work.

Short story A short work of narrative fiction whose plot, characters, settings, point of view, style, and theme reinforce each other, often in subtle ways, creating an overall unity.

Stream of consciousness A narrative technique primarily based on the works of psychologist-philosophers Sigmund Freud, Henri Bergson, and William James, who originated the phrase in 1890. In fiction, the technique is designed to represent a character's inner thoughts, which flow in a stream without grammatical structure and punctuation or apparent coherence. The novels *Ulysses* and *Finnegans Wake,* by James Joyce, contain the most famous and celebrated use of the technique. Stream of consciousness, which represents the borders of consciousness, may be distinguished from the interior monologue, which is more structured and rational.

Structure The organizational pattern or relation among the parts of a story. Questions to help determine a story's structure may include the following: Is the story told without stop from beginning to end, or is it divided into sections? Does the narrator begin at the beginning of a plot, or when actions are already under way (*in medias res,* in the middle of things)? Does the narrator begin at the end of the plot and tell the story through a series of flashbacks? Is the story organized by major events or episodes, or by images or moods?

Style   One of the elements of fiction, style in a literary work refers to the diction (choice of words), syntax (arrangement of words), and other linguistic features of a work. Just as no two people have identical fingerprints or voices, so no two writers use words in exactly the same way. Style distinguishes one writer's language from another's.

Symbol   A reference to a concrete image, object, character, pattern, or action whose associations evoke significant meanings beyond the literal ones. An archetype, or archetypal symbol, is a symbol whose associations are said to be universal – that is, they extend beyond the locale of a particular nation or culture. Religious symbols, such as the cross, are of this kind.

In literature, *symbolism* refers to an author's use of symbols.

Theme   One of the elements of fiction, the theme is the main idea that is explored in a story. Characters, plot, settings, point of view, and style all contribute to a theme's development.

Third-person narrator   See **point of view.**

Tone   Like tone of voice. Literary tone is determined by the attitude of a narrator toward characters in a story and the story's readers. For example, the tone of a work may be impassioned, playful, haughty, grim, or matter-of-fact. Tone is distinct from atmosphere, which refers to the mood of a story and can be analyzed as part of its setting.

Unity   The oneness of a short story. Generally, each of a story's elements has a unity of its own, and all reinforce each other to create an overall unity. Although a story's unity may be evident on first reading, much more often discovering the unity requires rereading, reflection, and analysis. Readers who engage themselves in these ways experience the pleasure of bringing a story to life.

About the Editor

Wyn Kelley (Ph.D., Stanford University) is a senior lecturer on the Literature Faculty at the Massachusetts Institute of Technology. She is the author of *Melville's City: Literary and Urban Form in Nineteenth-Century New York* (1996) and of essays in collections such as *Savage Eye: Melville and the Visual Arts* (1991), *Melville's Evermoving Dawn: Centennial Essays* (1997), *The Cambridge Companion to Herman Melville* (1998), *Ungraspable Phantom: Essays on* Moby-Dick (2006), *Melville and Women* (2006), and *Hawthorne and Melville: Writing Relationship* (2007). She has edited Blackwell Publishers' *A Companion to Herman Melville* (2006) and coedited with Jill Barnum and Christopher Sten "*Whole Oceans Away*": *Melville and the Pacific* (2006). She serves as associate editor of the Melville Society journal *Leviathan* and as founding member of the Melville Society Cultural Project.